In The Name Of Allah ﷻ, The Entirely Merciful, The Especially Merciful

ISLAMIC STUDIES

Student's Textbook

A Comprehensive International Curriculum

Grade Three
Part 1

International Curricula Organization

Islamic Studies Grade 3 - Student's Textbook, part 1

© **International Curricula Organization, 2020**

Team of authors
Islamic Studies : Students Texbook : Grade 3 / Team of authors.

ISBN : 9960-9681-5- 4
1 English Language - Islamic Studies   1 title
428,241 dc   1426/5251

L.D.No. 1426/5215

ISBN : 9960-9681-5-4

International Curricula Organization
Website: www.iconetwork.com
E-mail: info@iconetwork.com

 /iconetwork -   @iconetwork

تنزيل المحتوى الصوتي لكتب التربية الإسلامية من خلال الرابط التالي:

www.iconetwork.com/islamic-audio/

أو

الباركود (QR)

Acknowledgment

While the hard work of all participants in this project deserves recognition, it is however necessary to acknowledge the invaluable contributions of those, who at the helm of affairs, selflessly devoted all their faculties to navigating this project to fruition and for whom this undertaking was indeed a labor of love.

Members of the Educational Committee

Members of the Technical Committee

Members of the Islamic Studies Committee

Members of the Quality control Committee

Members of the Editing Committee

Team of Authors

Dr. Qadir Abdus Sabur, USA

Paul Opoku Addae, United Kingdom

Ashraf Ajam, South Africa

Abdel-Salam Al-Drouby, United Kingdom

Talib Baker, South Africa

Moegamat Yusuf Feltman, South Africa

Saleem Hassan, United Kingdom

Abdullah Jeena, South Africa

Muhammad Adeel Samodien, South Africa

Abdullah Al-Badri, Saudi Arabia

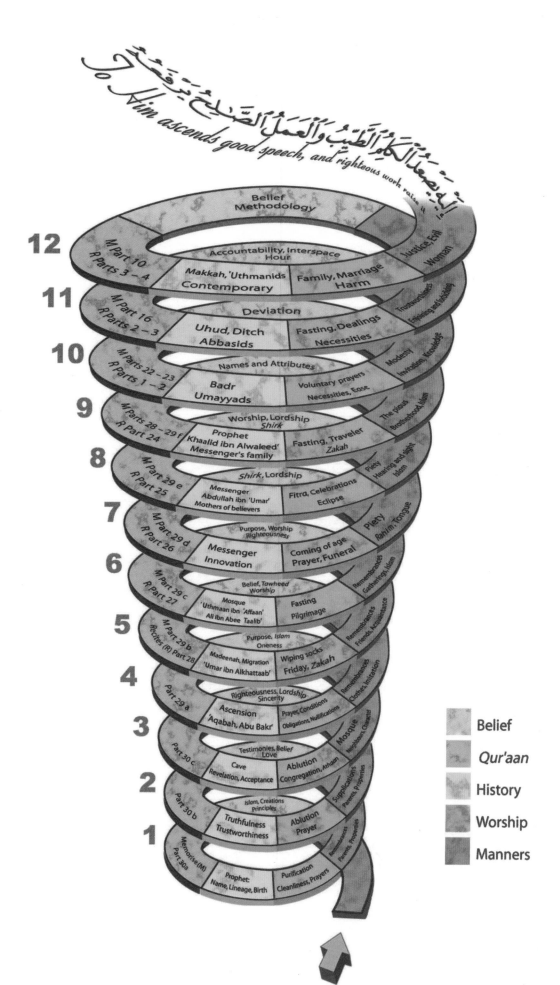

To Him ascends good speech, and righteous work raise it.

تَرَفَعُهُ ٱلْعَمَلُ ٱلصَّالِحُ وَٱلْكَلِمُ ٱلطَّيِّبُ يَصْعَدُ إِلَيْهِ

12
M Part 10
R Parts 3 – 4

Belief
Methodology

Accountability, Interspace
Hour

Makkah, 'Uthmanids
Contemporary

Family, Marriage
Harm

Justice, Evil

Woman

11
M Part 16
R Parts 2 – 3

Deviation

Uhud, Ditch
Abbasids

Fasting, Dealings
Necessities

Trustworthiness

Enjoining evil, forbidding

10
M Parts 22 – 23
R Parts 1 – 2

Names and Attributes

Badr
Umayyads

Voluntary prayers
Necessities, Ease

Modesty

Invitation, Knowledge

9
M Parts 28 – 29 f
R Part 24

Worship, Lordship
Shirk

Prophet
Khaalid ibn Alwaleed'
Messenger's family

Fasting, Traveler
Zakah

The pious

Brotherhood, Islam

8
M Part 29 e
R Part 25

Shirk, Lordship

Messenger
Abdullah ibn 'Umar'
Mothers of believers

Fitra, Celebrations
Eclipse

Piety

Hearing and sight, Islam

7
M Part 29 d
R Part 26

Purpose, Worship
Righteousness

Messenger
Innovation

Coming of age
Prayer, Funeral

Piety

Rahim, Tongue

6
M Part 29 c
R Part 27

Belief, Tawheed
Worship

Mosque
'Uthmaan ibn 'Affaan'
Ali ibn Abee Taalib'

Fasting
Pilgrimage

Remembrances
Gatherings, Islam

5
M Part 29 b
Recites (R) Part 28

Purpose, Islam
Oneness

Madeenah, Migration
'Umar ibn Alkhattaab'

Wiping socks
Friday, Zakah

Remembrances
Friends, Acceptance

4
Part 29 a

Righteousness, Lordship
Sincerity

Ascension
'Aqabah, Abu Bakr'

Prayer, Conditions
Obligations, Nullifications

Remembrances
Clothes, Imitation

3
Part 30 c

Testimonies, Belief
Love

Cave
Revelation, Acceptance

Ablution
Congregation, Athaan

Mosque
Neighbours, Character

2
Part 30 b

Islam, Creations
principles

Truthfulness
Trustworthiness

Ablution
Prayer

Supplications
Parents, Properties

1
Memorise (M)
Part 30 a

Prophet:
Name, Lineage, Birth

Purification
Cleanliness, Prayers

Remembrances
Parents, Properties

Belief

Qur'aan

History

Worship

Manners

Introduction

In the name of Allah, the Entirely Merciful, the Especially Merciful. All praise is for Allah ﷻ alone whose help and forgiveness we seek. We ask for His protection against evil and wrongdoing. Whomever Allah ﷻ guides cannot be misguided and whomever Allah allows to go astray cannot be guided to the straight path. I bear witness that there is no god worthy of worship but Allah ﷻ, without partners, and I bear witness that Muhammad ﷺ is His messenger.

Rationale and Objectives

Education is perhaps the most influential social institution in any society. The role of schooling is to transmit a common set of beliefs, values, norms, and ways of understanding from the adult members of a society to its youth. Muslims worldwide share a common set of values based on the *Qur'aan* and the *Sunnah* of Prophet Muhammad ﷺ. It is the function of Islamic schools to teach these values to Muslim students through the use of well-designed curricula.

The International Curricula Organization has undertaken the task of developing Arabic and Islamic studies curricula that could be used by Islamic schools all over the world. The overall objectives of these curricula are to:

- Provide a framework for instruction in Arabic and Islamic studies for English - speaking schools;
- Assist young Muslims in learning the issues and practices of the religion of Islam, thus imparting to them beliefs, values, norms and ways of understanding based on Islamic teachings;
- Instruct young Muslims in Arabic – the language of the Glorious *Qur'aan*;
- Provide a knowledge base that could help young Muslims maintain their Islamic

  identity.

A committee of Muslim scholars met the challenge of designing the syllabus as part of the groundwork for developing textbooks. The initial work entailed a study of the nature of Muslim life in Muslim societies of the world, providing valuable insights into the differences in social practices and traditions. Based on their analysis the instructional content was arranged in the following order: 1) *'Aqeedah* (Islamic Doctrine), 2) The Glorious *Qur'aan* and its sciences, 3) The *Sunnah*, *Seerah* (Biography of the Prophet ﷺ and History), 4) Acts of worship and dealings, and 5) Morals and manners. These five areas of emphasis are detailed at each grade level.

Organization of this book

The entire curriculum is organized by grade level. Each grade level is subdivided into twenty – nine units and each unit has three forty-minute lessons. The five instructional content areas are presented using a spiral approach in which students revisit the content area and study it in greater depth each year (see graphical representation on the previous page). Throughout the text, there are integrated review units. These units require students to draw upon all of the instructional material presented previously across the content area.

Effective implementation of this curriculum

The twenty-nine units contained in this book were designed to cover two semesters. It is recommended that three lessons be covered each week.. The syllabus designers recognize that individual schools are structured differently. In schools in which three lessons per week is the norm, the implementation of the curriculum is straightforward. However, some schools may have Islamic studies classes everyday. In those instances, the additional two classes could be used for supplementary *Qur'aanic* recitation practice. Since each lesson contains exercises and activities, which are sufficient for a forty - minute lesson, additional weekly class sessions could also be used for enrichment using these additional activities. Field trips to sacred sites, browsing online Islamic web sites, as well as organized group activities could also be used to enrich the educational experiences of students. Additional enrichment activities may also be found on our web site www.iconetwork.com.

Review and Evaluation

While every effort has been made to ensure that the contents of this book is accurate and that it complies with the highest standards, we welcome any comments, suggestions, and critical evaluation that would assist in further developing this book. To contribute to the development of this project, please complete the questionnaire posted on our website at: www.iconetwork.com.

International Curricula

CONTENTS

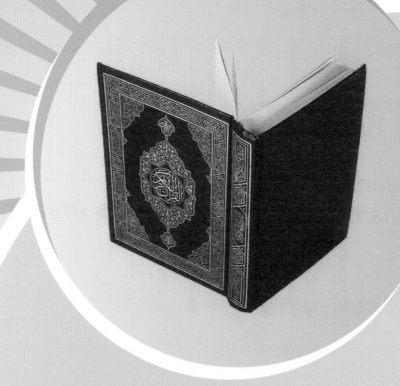

Unit 1

- The Meaning of *Ihsaan*

- The Status and Importance of *Ihsaan*

- Etiquettes of Reading the *Qur'aan: Tahaarah*

The Meaning of
Ihsaan

Word Bank

Ihsaan
muhsin

What is *Ihsaan*?

- *Ihsaan* means doing something in the best possible way. It also means to do good to others.

- The Messenger of Allah ﷺ said that *Ihsaan* means to worship Allah ﷻ, as if one can see Him. If one is unable to do this, then one should know that Allah ﷻ is always watching.

- *Deen* (religion) has three levels: *Islam, Iman,* and *Ihsaan*. They are connected to each other and *Ihsaan* is the highest of the three. Having *Ihsaan* means that the person already has *Islam* and *Iman*.

● If a person can worship Allah ﷻ as if he sees Him, or knows that Allah ﷻ is watching him, then this person has *Ihsaan*. Such a person will:
  - Not do anything wrong,
  - Not harm anybody,
  - Act with goodness,
  - Try to do his/her best in every deed,
  - Accurately follow the teachings of Islam in all his/her affairs.

● A person who has *Ihsaan* is known as a *muhsin*. A *muhsin* is aware that Allah ﷻ is always watching; at night, during the day, in private, and in public.

● A *muhsin* is good to others by using his/her:
  - body   - wealth   - position   - knowledge.

- To have *Ihsaan* a person must make sure that:
  - His intention is pure and clean. This means that the person should do things only for the sake of Allah. No good deed should be done to show off be famous, or for money.
  - Actions should be according to Allah's guidance in the *Qur'aan* and the Prophet's *Sunnah*.

1- Look at your lesson text and fill in the blanks:

- *Ihsaan* means to do something in the ..b.est.. possible way and to do ...good to ..others..... .

- The Messenger of Allah said that *Ihsaan* is to worship Allah as if one can .....See......... Him.

- If one is unable to do that, then one should know that Allah is always .Watching.

2- Mention the three levels of *deen* (religion).

The 3 levels of deen are Ihsan Iman Islam.

3- From your knowledge of the previous lessons, **list** the pillars of *Islam* and *Iman*.

Write it down on a piece of paper then turn it over. Your teacher will then give you the answers. Check your answers against those of your teacher.

Piers of Iman

1- blive in Allah
2- blive in Angels
3- blive in Allah's bok
4- blive in the messengers of Allah
5- blive in the day of Judgment.

Piers of Islam

1- Hajj
2- fasting
3- Shahaddah
4- Prayer
5- Givig money to poor pepoles.

6- blive in the good or bad.

Activity 1

Answer the following questions:

1- What is the second level of *deen* (religion).

Islam, Iman, Ihsan

2- To do things only for Allah ﷻ is called *ikhlaas*. In English *ikhlaas* means to be

having a sincer intionton Their muslims
is pure if the acts are done for the sake
of Allah as he will Reward him/her

3- In **Ihsaan**, who should Muslims worship as if they can see Him?

Allah

4- Who is watching all the time?

Allah

5- A person who has *Ihsaan* will not .... anybody.

A person who has inscan will not
hurt anybody.

A person continues to sin. When a Muslim advises him, he says that people do not see him or know anything about him.

In groups of three, discuss and make notes on how a Muslim can use *Ihsaan* to deal with this situation.
How would he/she advise this person?
Remember the four things mentioned in the lesson that a *muhsin* can use to show goodness to people.

Give a short presentation on how your group would deal with the situation.

The Status and Importance of *Ihsaan*

Word Bank

virtuous
requirement
commanded
advisable

How important is *Ihsaan*?

- *Ihsaan* is a very important part of Islam.

- *Ihsaan* is the highest of the three levels of *deen* (religion). It is higher than *Iman* and *Islam*. To reach *Ihsaan,* it is necessary to have *Islam*, and Iman.

- *Ihsaan* is very important like the two basic requirements: *Islam* and *Iman*.

Iman   Islam

Ihsaan

Islam

Highest Level

Iman

Islam

Middle Level

Islam

Lower Level

Amuslim has it when he reaches the highest level of *Iman*.

● Allah ﷻ commands Muslims to act with *Ihsaan*. The following three a*ayaat* are examples of this.

Allah ﷻ says,

" *And do good; indeed Allah loves the doers of good.*" *(Soorah al-Baqarah:* 195)

● In this *aayah,* Allah ﷻ tells Muslims to act with *Ihsaan* and that He loves those who act with *Ihsaan*.

Allah ﷻ says,

"*Indeed Allah orders justice and good conduct.*" *(Soorah an-Nahl:* 90)

In this *aayah* Allah ﷻ command the believers act with *Ihsaan*.

● In this *aayah*, Allah ﷻ also commands Muslims to act with *Ihsaan*.

"Worship Allah and associate nothing with Him, and to parents do good, and to relatives, orphans, the needy, the near neighbor, the neighbor farther away, the companion at your side, the traveller…"

(*Soorah an-Nisaa'*: 36)

Here, Allah ﷻ mentions a list of people with whom one should act with *Ihsaan*.

● The Prophet ﷺ has also attached great importance to *Ihsaan*. He said:

"Allah ﷻ has prescribed Ihsaan in everything (we do)."

(Muslim)

Exercises

1- **Explain** how we can say that *Ihsaan* is the highest of the three levels of *deen*.

Ihsan is the hist level of deen because Ihsan has more of Allah's words

2- **Soorah** al-Baqarah, aayah 195, is mentioned in the lesson.
Why is it mentioned in this lesson?

....

....

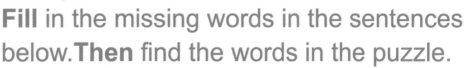

Activity 1

Fill in the missing words in the sentences below. **Then** find the words in the puzzle.

1- Allah ﷻ loves the doers of ..good..............

2- Allah ﷻ ..Orders......... justice and good conduct.

3- Allah ﷻ issues a strict ..camend.. to the believers.

4- In order to have *Ihsaan* a person must have *Iman* and .....Islam...........

5- *Ihsaan* is higher than .....Iman... and *Islam*.

- **Your** teacher will divide you into three groups. Page two of your lesson contains three *aayaat* and each *aayah* has a short explanation.

- **Your** teacher will allocate one *aayah*, together with its explanation, to each group.

- **As** a group, read the *aayah* and its explanation aloud. Practice saying it perfectly as a group.

- **Towards** the end of the lesson, each group will have a chance to read out their section.

- **Let's** see who does it the best!

Etiquettes of Reading the *Qur'aan*: **Tahaarah**

Word Bank

tahaarah
(cleanliness)

taahir
(pure and clean)

Before reciting the Qur'aan, a Muslim should be *taahir* (pure and clean)

- Islam requires *tahaarah* (cleanliness). One of the acts of worship that needs *wudoo'*, is reading the *Qur'aan*.

Allah ﷻ says,

"Allah loves those who are constantly repentant and loves those who purify themselves."

(*Soorah al-Baqarah*: 222)

- Before Muslims touch the *Qur'aan* they should have *wudoo'*. Reciting the *Qur'aan* is an *'ibaadah* (form of worship), and it is the best form of *dhikr*.

- The place where one recites the *Qur'aan* should also be clean. Muslims should not read or recite the *Qur'aan* in the bathroom.

- The *Qur'aan* is the words of Allah, ﷻ and Muslims must respect it.

- The Prophet ﷺ said in a letter to the Muslims of Yemen, *"No one should touch the Qur'aan except with wudoo'."* In other words you must have *wudoo'* before touching the *Qur'aan*

Exercises!

Answer the questions:

1- What should Muslims do before they touch the *Qur'aan*?

....

....

....

....

2- It is good to recite the *Qur'aan* because it is the best form of.............................

3- In which types of places should Muslims not recite the *Qur'aan*?
Give three examples.

....

....

....

....

Which places are recommended for Muslims to recite the *Qur'aan*?
Look at the pictures below:

What did Allah's Messenger ﷺ mention in his letter to the Muslims of Yemen?
Write down the answer.
What can Muslims learn from it?

_____

_____

_____

_____

_____

_____

_____

_____

_____

_____

Unit 2

The Merits of Ihsaan

Word Bank

encourage
merits
virtues
taqwaa (piety)

What are the merits and virtues of *Ihsaan*?

- Many merits of *Ihsaan* are mentioned in the *Qur'aan* and the *Sunnah*. Some of these merits are mentioned below. Allah ﷻ rewards the person who acts with *Ihsaan*.

Allah ﷻ says,

"Be patient, for indeed, Allah does not allow to be lost the reward of those who do good (Ihsaan)."

(Soorah Hood: 115)

- Allah is ﷻ with those who do *Ihsaan*.

Allah ﷻ says,

> *"Indeed Allah is with those who fear Him and who are doers of good (Ihsaan)."*
>
> *(Soorah an-Nahl: 128)*

- Allah's ﷻ mercy is near to the *muhsin*[1].

Allah ﷻ says,

> *"Indeed the Mercy of Allah is near to the doers of good (Ihsaan.)"*
>
> *(Soorah al-A'raaf: 56)*

- Many other benefits of *Ihsaan* can be mentioned. Some of them are:
  - It creates love for Allah ﷻ in the heart of a *muhsin*.
  - The *muhsin* will be free from fear and sadness in the Hereafter.
  - It brings the *muhsin* closer to Allah ﷻ.
  - It develops *taqwaa* (piety) in a Muslim.
  - It keeps people sincere.
  - It improves the conditions of the society.
  - It spreads love and unity among Muslims.

---

1. See page 3 for an explanation of muhsin.

Exercises!

1- Mention five merits of *Ihsaan*.

1- It creates love for Allah in the heart of an mohsin.

2- in spreeds love and unity among mosrims.

3- it keeps pepole sincere

4- it brings the mohsin closer to Allah.

5- it improved the conditains of the socity.

2- In this lesson, what would explain to you the kindness of Allah ﷻ with the believers?

Allah is kind to pepole even none brivers He is so merciful then nobne he is NOT alike to anyone.

Activity 1

In groups, discuss the following:
- *Taqwaa* means being aware of Allah ﷻ and being fearful of the displeasure of Allah ﷻ. How does *Ihsaan* develop *taqwaa*?
- **How** does *Ihsaan* keep people sincere?
- **How** does a community or society improve through *Ihsaan*?

At home write down your answers to the same questions and submit this to your teacher the following day.

Activity 2

In groups of three:
- **Design** a poster that lists the merits of *Ihsaan*.
- **Make** it as interesting and colorful as possible.
- **Continue** with your project during your free time at school or at home.
- **Present** your poster to the class by the following week.

Ihsaan at All Times

Word Bank
stranger
'ibaadah
concentrate
dedicated

To have Ihsaan at all times

- A Muslim should have *Ihsaan* at all times. He/she should have *Ihsaan* at school, at home, while working, with friends, with family, or even with strangers.

- *Ihsaan* is of great importance when engaging in any *'ibaadah* (worship of Allah ﷻ). Muslims should try to worship Allah ﷻ as if they can see Him. If this is not possible then they should realize that Allah ﷻ is watching. If a Muslim does this, then his her prayer will improve, because he/she will always be aware of Allah ﷻ. For

example, Muslims will not play during prayer because they know that Allah ﷻ is watching them. They will rather concentrate and be more dedicated in worship.

- Muslims should show *Ihsaan* to all people at all times. They should show *Ihsaan* to the rich and poor, the young and the old, the good and the bad, and Muslims and non-Muslims.

- The Prophet ﷺ always practiced *Ihsaan*, even when someone harmed him. An example of this is what happened to the Prophet ﷺ. They even harmed his body. Even though the Prophet ﷺ was hurt and sad, he still prayed for the guidance of those that did this wrong. He did not pray for their punishment.

- *Ihsaan* should be shown to:

  parents, wives, husbands, children, relatives, orphans, the poor, travellers, employees, teachers, people in general.

- A Muslim should always behave with *Ihsaan*. During times of difficulty and ease, *Ihsaan* must always be there.

● Animals should also be cared for with *Ihsaan*.

● The Messenger of Allah 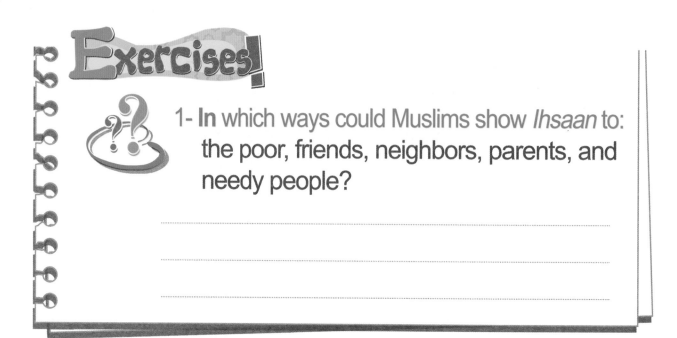 narrated the following story: "One day, a man walking in the road became very thirsty. He found a well and he went down into it. He drank and then came out. He saw a panting dog eating the wet soil out of thirst. The man said, "This dog is as thirsty as I was." He then went down the well and filled his shoe with water. He held the shoe in his hand and let the dog drink from it. He was grateful to Allah and he was forgiven." The companions of the Prophet said, "Do we get reward for the way we deal with animals?" He replied: "There is reward for dealing kindly with every living being." (Muslim).

Exercises!

1- **In** which ways could Muslims show *Ihsaan* to: the poor, friends, neighbors, parents, and needy people?

....

....

....

2- **Explain** what is meant by "*Ihsaan* during worship".

....

....

Activity 1

Write a short composition on any one of the following topics:

a) Cruelty to animals is forbidden in Islam.

b) An incident where I behaved with *Ihsaan* towards an animal.

Your composition should be no less than 50 words in length. Plan it in class and complete it at home. Ask your parents for some suggestions.

....

....

....

....

....

Submit this to your teacher the following day.

Activity 2

Over the next five days, complete the following form at the end of each day. It is for your self-evaluation. You do not need to show it to any of your friends. After five days, check and see where you can improve. Ask your parents how you can improve.

Simply enter a check sign ✓ if you think you made a big effort to have *Ihsaan* in any of the listed actions. If there was no big effort or if you cannot remember, then enter a circle.

Example

Day/ Date	Fajr	Dhuhr	'Asr	Maghrib	'Ishaa	Parents	Friends	Animals	The Poor	Think of Allah At Any Other Time. Name the Occasion
Friday 20/11	✓	O	✓	✓	O	✓	✓	O	✓	O

Unit 2

The *Siwaak*

Word Bank

miswaak
siwaak
Araak Tree

Before reciting the *Qur'aan* it is recommended that Muslims use a *siwaak*

- Muslims use the *siwaak* to clean the mouth. It is also called a *miswaak*. It keeps the mouth fresh and Muslims are encouraged to use it before reading the *Qur'aan*. The *siwaak* is often taken from the *Araak tree*. The companion of the Prophet ﷺ, Ibn Mas'ood ؓ said, "I used to gather sticks from the *Araak tree* for the Messenger of Allah ﷺ." (Ahmad)

- The Messenger of Allah ﷺ said, "The *siwaak* is a way

to clean the mouth
and please the Lord."
(Al-Bukhaari)
When Muslims read
the *Qur'aan* and use
the *siwaak*, they please Allah ﷻ.

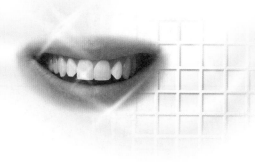

● The Prophet ﷺ said that using the *siwaak* is one of
   the practices of the *fitrah* (natural way). (Muslim)

● Using the *siwaak* is a form of worship which is easy
   to perform.
   The Prophet ﷺ used the *siwaak*:
   1- Before each prayer.
   2- Before reading the *Qur'aan*.
   3- Before sleeping.
   4- When waking up.
   5- During fasting.

● Allah's Messenger ﷺ said, "If it were not that
   I would burden my *ummah*, I would have
   commanded them to use the *siwaak* before every
   prayer." (Al-Bukhaari and Muslim)

Exercises!

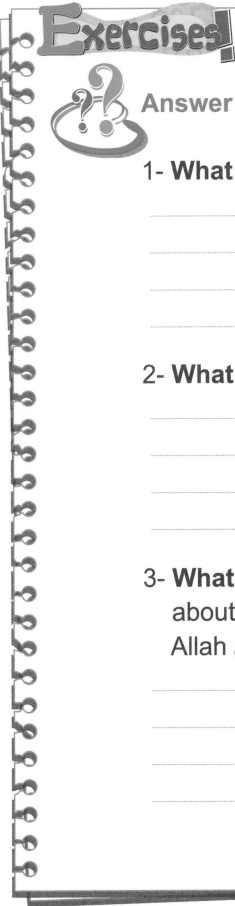

Answer the questions:

1- **What** is a *siwaak*?

....

....

....

2- **What** is the *Araak* Tree?

....

....

....

3- **What** did the Messenger of Allah ﷺ say about using the *siwaak* and pleasing Allah ﷻ?

....

....

....

Activity 1

When did the Prophet ﷺ use the *siwaak*?
Circle the correct answers.

Before going to the toilet

For every prayer

Before reading the *Qur'aan*

For every *Du'aa*   ○

When waking up

During playing

Before sleeping   ○

After reading a book

During fasting

When angry

Discuss

Look at the picture below and tick those things which can be used to clean the mouth:

Unit 3

- The Meaning of *Rabb*

- Signs of the *Rabb*

- Beautifying the Voice when Reciting the *Qur'aan*

The Meaning of Rabb

Word Bank

Rabb (Lord), Lordship,

What does Rabb mean? Who is the Rabb?

- The Arabic word 'Rabb' is often taken as 'Lord.' 'Lord,' in English means one who rules over others.

- The word 'Rabb' however, means much more. "Rabb" refers to Allah ﷻ as the one:
  - Who is worshipped.
  - Who rules over the creation.
  - Who is the Creator of everything.
  - Who is the Owner of everything.
  - Who is the Provider for all.

- Allah ﷻ is the *Rabb* and He is the only one who controls the creation.

- Allah ﷻ is the creator of everything. Humanity, the universe, the earth, animals, birds, fish, the mountains, water and air, are all creations of Allah ﷻ.

- Allah ﷻ is the true owner of everything. He is also the provider for all of His creation. Everything that people have, is given to them by Allah ﷻ, and He can take it away at any time. People will also be held accountable for the way they used the things that Allah ﷻ gave them.

- Allah ﷻ rules over everything. He has the power and wisdom to do anything. His law cannot be changed and has to be obeyed.

 1- **What** is the difference in meaning between the words 'Lord' and '*Rabb*'?

done in class

Rabb Refers To Allah as the one Who is worshiped Allah is the porvider oner of everything, corater of Every Thing,

Who Rules over The station

 2- **Name** five great creations of Allah ﷻ and explain why they are great. Also mention how they show the Lordship of Allah ﷻ.

1- Allah is the crator
2- Allah is the porvider
3- one to be worshiped
4- Allah one
5- Gived us our clothes

Activity 1

Work in small groups. Some people think that there are others, besides Allah ﷻ, who can share in His Lordship over creation. **Give** a few examples of this:

He is The The you'
He is the oner of evrything
The providor of all creation

Activity 2

Your teacher will divide you into groups of four.

In your groups:

- **Discuss** why Allah ﷻ is the only true *Rabb*.
- **Summarize** your discussions into five points.
- **One** person from your group will be asked to read the 5 points to the class.

Signs of the *Rabb*

Word Bank

signs
vast
magnificence
system

Recognizing the *Rabb* through His signs

- People may recognize their *Rabb*, Allah ﷻ through His creation.

- Muslims see the vastness, the magnificence, the exactness, the system and the perfection of the creation of Allah ﷻ. When they see it, it is clear to them that:
  - There must be a Wise Creator;
  - There must be an Owner of the entire creation;
  - There must be someone All-Knowing who rules over it;
  - There must be someone who provides for everything;

- There must be someone who keeps the system running;
- That someone is Allah ﷺ, their *Rabb*.

- People can see the Greatness, Power, and Lordship of Allah ﷺ in His creation, from the ant to the stars.

- Some of Allah's ﷺ signs in His creation, however, make people more easily aware of the *Rabb*. Among them are:
  - The vastness of the universe
  - Minute atoms
  - The stars and th
  - The Earth and t planets
  - The system in t universe
  - The occurrenc and day
  - The way clouds form and rain falls
  - The way plants grow
  - The seas, rivers, mountains and trees
  - The animals, fish, birds, insects etc.
  - The human being

[handwritten note: Mana]

[handwritten note: Minute atoms are so funny]

1- **When** people see the vastness and beauty of the creation, what should it make them aware of?

Shoul be awar of There rabb.

2- **Besides** the creations listed in your lesson, think of other creations of Allah ﷻ and put one into each empty shape.

Allah's ﷻ creation

Khadeejah tore up her homework sheet by accident and threw it away. She thought it was garbage.

When she realized it was not garbage, she brought it back.

There was one piece missing and one big stain on it. Can you help her solve the 'word search!'

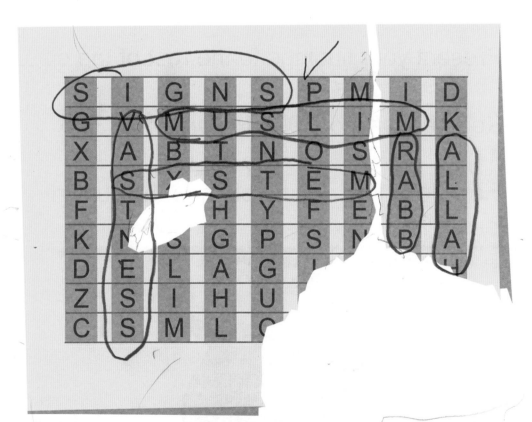

S	I	G	N	S	P	M	I	D
G	V	M	U	S	L	I	M	K
X	A	B	T	N	O	S	R	A
B	S	Y	S	T	E	M	A	L
F	T		H	Y	F	E	B	L
K	N		G	P	S	N	B	A
D	E	L	A	G				H
Z	S	I	H	U				
C	S	M	L	O				

RABB   SIGNS   VASTNESS

SYSTEM   ALLAH   MUSLIM

Activity 2

In pairs or small groups:

1- Decide on any one creation of Allah ﷻ.

   - Discuss the ways that this creation shows the Lordship of Allah ﷻ.

   - Present your findings to the rest of the class.

2- Read *aayah* No. 190 of *soorah* No. 3.

   - How does this *aayah* relate to the current lesson?

Beautifying the Voice when Reciting the Qur'aan

Word Bank

beautify
melodically
mellow
melodiously
tilaawah
(recitation)

Muslims should recite the *Qur'aan* in a mellow voice.

- When reciting the *Qur'aan*, a Muslim should make sure that the *tilaawah* is correct. Regular repetition helps a Muslim learn the corrrect *tilaawah*.

- It is pleasing to hear the *Qur'aan* being recited in a melodious voice, and it makes it easier to memorize the *Qur'aan* well.

- The Prophet ﷺ has mentioned the merits of reciting the *Qur'aan* in a beautiful voice.

> He said, *"Indeed the best of people with regard to voices, is he whom you feel fears Allah ﷻ when he recites [the Qur'aan]."* (Ad-Daarimi)

> He also said , *"Beautify the Qur'aan with your voices, for indeed, the voice of beauty increases the beauty of the Qur'aan."* (Haakim)

- It is important that a Muslim recites the *Qur'aan* melodically because:
  1- The Prophet ﷺ used to recite, in a mellow and tranquil manner.
  2- The Prophet ﷺ said:

> *"Whoever does not sweeten the Qur'aan (recite it melodiously) is not of us."* (Al-Bukhaari)

  3- It is pleasing to hear and it helps a Muslim to memorize more of the *Qur'aan*.

- A Muslim should learn the *Qur'aan* from a good reciter who can correct his recitation.

- Muslims should not sing the *Qur'aan* like music. This takes a Muslim away from being sincere in reciting, and from the correct *tilaawah* of the *Qur'aan*.

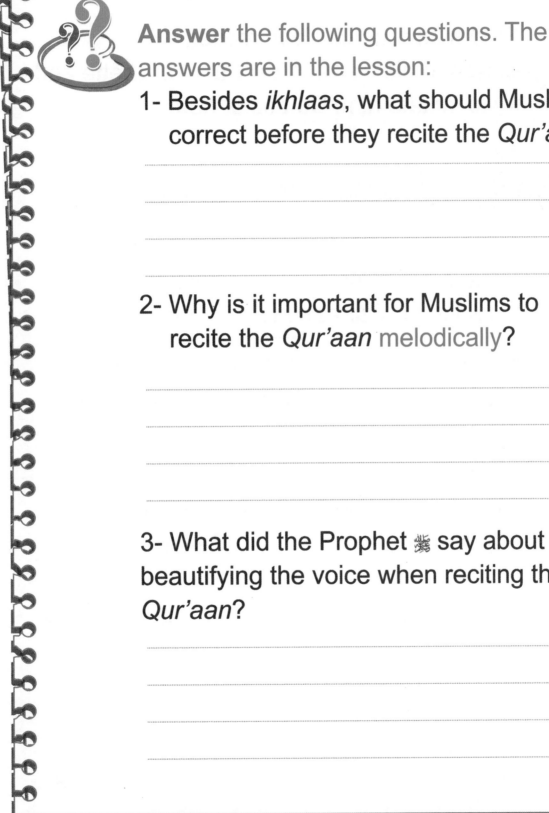

Answer the following questions. The answers are in the lesson:

1- Besides *ikhlaas*, what should Muslims correct before they recite the *Qur'aan*?

....

....

....

2- Why is it important for Muslims to recite the *Qur'aan* melodically?

....

....

....

....

3- What did the Prophet ﷺ say about beautifying the voice when reciting the *Qur'aan*?

....

....

....

....

Activity 1

Find a famous *Qur'aan* reciter.
Listen to his *tilaawah* on CD or cassette and try to imitate him. Do this at home.

Activity 2

Make a list of the reasons why it is important to recite the *Qur'aan* melodically.

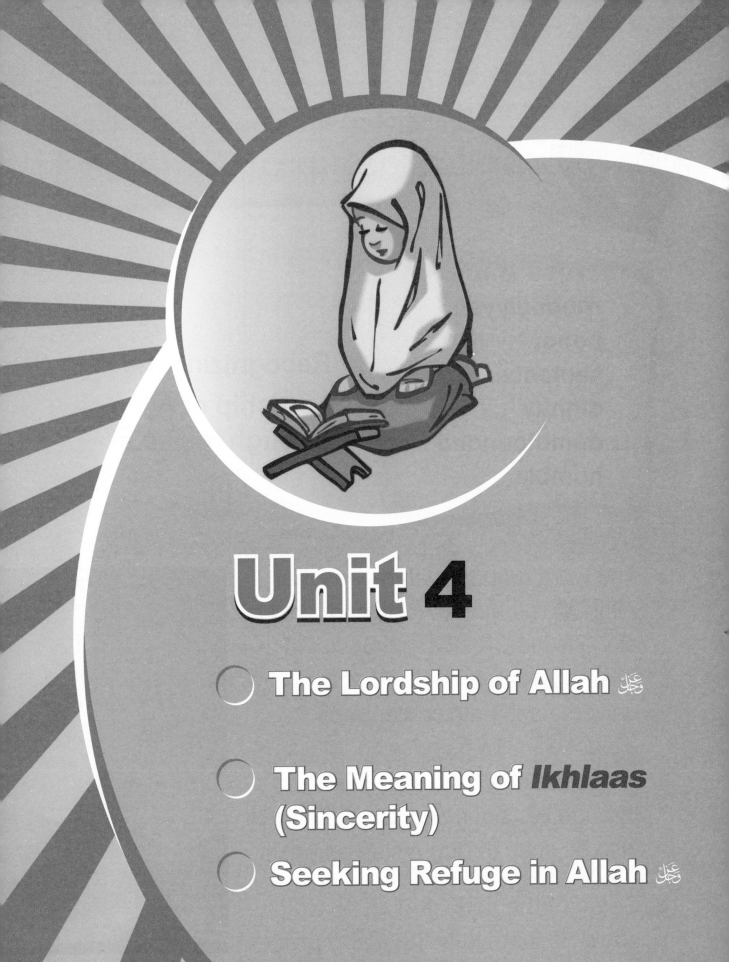

Unit 4

- The Lordship of Allah عَزَّ وَجَلَّ

- The Meaning of *Ikhlaas* (Sincerity)

- Seeking Refuge in Allah عَزَّ وَجَلَّ

The Lordship of Allah ﷻ

Word Bank

ruboobiyyah
honor
sentence
dignity
dumbfounded
humble

Recognizing the Lordship of Allah ﷻ through His acts

- The word *ruboobiyyah* means that Allah ﷻ is the only *Rabb* and that He alone is the Creator and Sustainer. Allah ﷻ alone is the Lord of the universe and nothing happens except with His permission. Muslims recognize that Allah ﷻ is the *Rabb* through His signs and creation. It can also be seen through Allah's ﷻ acts.

- Some of the acts of Allah ﷻ which show us that He is the *Rabb are*:

a) Allah ﷻ is the Creator of everything,

b) Allah ﷻ owns everything,

c) Allah ﷻ gives people blessings,

d) Allah ﷻ causes things to happen,

e) Allah ﷻ gives life and takes it away,

f) Allah ﷻ gives and takes honor and dignity,

g) Allah ﷻ does not leave us alone,

h) Allah ﷻ controls everything.

- The One who does all these things is the only One who deserves to be worshipped.
  Prophet Ibraaheem عليه السلام was called by the king and questioned about his beliefs.
  Ibraheem said:
  "My Lord is the one who gives life and death."
  The King replied :
  "I also give life and death."
  The king then called his guards and ordered them to bring a man who had been sentenced to death. He then set this man free. Then he sent the guards to catch any man off the streets and bring him. When they returned he ordered that the man be killed, and it was done. The king then said that this was proof that he gave life and death.
  Ibraaheem عليه السلام said: "My Lord is the One who makes the sun rise in the East, so (if you are lord) then (try and) make it rise in the West."

The king was dumbfounded, as he did not know what to say. He could not do this. Only Allah ﷻ has the Power to make the sun rise.

● Muslims should worship their *Rabb*. This is done by:
a) Obeying His Orders,
b) Being humble to Him in their actions,
c) Keeping away from all things which He warned them of.

This is done when feeling:

a) His Greatness,   b) His Highness,
c) Fear of Him, and   d) Hope in His Mercy.

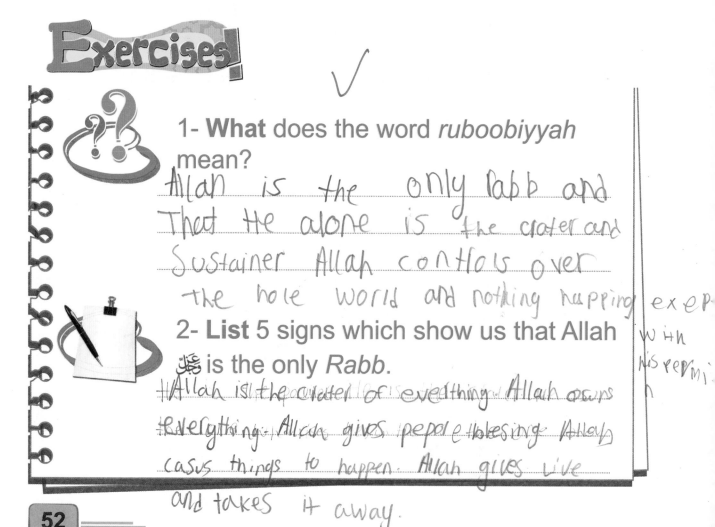

1- **What** does the word *ruboobiyyah* mean?

Allah is the only Rabb and That He alone is the crater and Sustainer Allah contHols over the hole world and nothing happing exep with his permi

2- **List** 5 signs which show us that Allah ﷻ is the only *Rabb*.

Allah is the crater of everything Allah owns Everything. Allah gives pepole blesing Allah casus things to happen. Allah gives live and takes it away.

In the story of Ibraaheem ﷺ and the king, what do you think of the king's argument and demonstration that he also gives life and death?

a) **Discuss** this in your groups.

b) **At home**, write down your answers and give them to the teacher before the coming lesson.

Activity 2

How would you explain to other people that Allah ﷻ is the Lord of the universe, that He controls everything and that only He should be worshipped?

Work in pairs:

a) **Discuss** and make notes of the things that are important to explain.

b) **Tell** the other groups in class what you think are the most important things to explain to a non-Muslim.

How could you explain that Allah ﷻ is the only Lord, Creator, and Sustainer of creation?

Unit 4

Lesson 2

The Meaning of *Ikhlaas* (Sincerity)

What is *ikhlaas*?

- In Islam, *ikhlaas* has to do with having a sincere intention. The Muslim's intention is pure if his acts are done for the sake of Allah ﷻ, in the hope that Allah ﷻ will reward him/her.

Word Bank

ikhlaas	intention
pure	motive
fulfill	rights

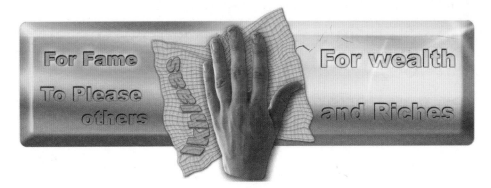

For Fame
To Please others
For wealth and Riches

- To do something only for the sake of Allah ﷻ means that whatever a person does should be only to seek Allah's ﷻ pleasure. Primarily, it should not be done with any other motive or intention.
Muslims must stay away from all forbidden things

and try to do all types of good and kind actions. They must fulfill everyone's rights in seeking Allah's ﷻ reward. If Muslims do it in this way, then they will please Allah ﷻ.

Muslims can gain *ikhlaas* by:

- Not showing off.
- Not doing good actions only for the purpose of gaining riches.
- Not doing anything for the sake of pleasing any creation. Muslims should do actions for the sake of pleasing Allah ﷻ and gaining His favor and blessings.

Whatever you do should be for the sake of Allah ﷻ

When you please your parents,
When you help a blind man across the street,
When you give a poor man *sadaqah*,
When you perform your *Salah*,
When you read the *Qur'aan* beautifully,
When you build a well in a poor land,
When you build a *masjid* in a faraway land,
When you earn money for your daily needs ...

All this must be only for the pleasure of Allah ﷻ and to seek the reward from Him alone.

1- **Write** down the meaning of *ikhlaas*.

has to do with having a sincer intintion the muslims'
intintion is pure if acts are done for the sake
of Allah in hope that Allah will rerod him/
her.

2- **Name** three ways in which Muslims can gain *ikhlaas*?

1. by reading salah

2. When yoo read the quran

3. When you give sdaqah.

3- **A man** gave some money in charity, and another man prayed in the *masjid*, but both of them did not get any reward from Allah ﷻ. Can you think of a few reasons why they were not rewarded for their actions.

because they raied ast.

See in Notebook!

they need

they tour money no money.

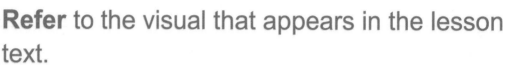

Activity 1

Refer to the visual that appears in the lesson text.

What do you understand by it?

Write down your explanation in no less than 50 words.

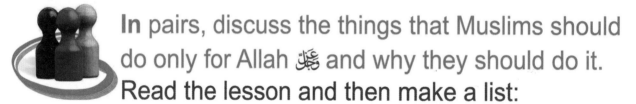

Activity 2

In pairs, discuss the things that Muslims should do only for Allah ﷻ and why they should do it.

Read the lesson and then make a list:

Seeking Refuge in Allah ﷻ

Word Bank

isti'aadhah (seeking refuge in Allah ﷻ), *Ar-Rajeem* (the accursed)

Muslims seek refuge in Allah ﷻ before they read the *Qur'aan*.

- Allah ﷻ instructs Muslims to seek refuge from the accursed enemy, *Shaytaan*, before reading the *Qur'aan*.

Allah ﷻ says,

"So when you recite the Qur'aan, [first] seek refuge in Allah from Satan, the expelled [from His Mercy]." (Soorah an-Nahl: 98)

Arabic	Transliteration	English meaning
أَعُوذُ بِاللهِ مِنَ الشَّيْطَانِ الرَّجِيمِ	A'oodhu billaahi min ash-Shaytaanir-Rajeem-	I seek refuge in Allah ﷻ from the accursed Shaytaan (Devil)

Isti'aadhah means,"I seek refuge in Allah ﷻ from the accursed Satan so that he cannot harm me or stop me from doing what I have been commanded, or make me do what I am not supposed to do." *Isti'aadhah* is to keep the evils of *Shaytaan* away. It prepares a Muslim to recite the *Qur'aan* by seeking Allah's ﷻ help. It also shows that a Muslim can defeat *Shaytaan* only with the help of Allah ﷻ. *Isti'aadhah* helps Muslims to:

1- be sincere in reciting   2- reflect on the meanings
3- understand the meaning   4- continue reading

Answer the following questions:

1- What does Allah ﷻ instruct Muslims to do before reciting the *Qur'aan*?

Sa Allah says A oodu bill abi min ash-Shaytani rajeem

2- What does *isti'aadhah* mean?
   See the table.

I seek refuge in Allah from the
accursed shaytaan (Devil).

Activity 1

List how the *isti'aadhah* helps Muslims before they read the *Qur'aan*.

What does '*Ar-Rajeem*' mean?

Ar-Rajeem means the accursed.
- islaahdaha Helps muslims get away
of shaytan and make   Intantion
to Allah as the way all

Activity 2

Listen to the *isti'aadhah* and practice it.

لَا مَعْبُودَ بِحَقٍّ إِلَّا الله

Unit 5

- The Significance of *Ikhlaas*

- The Importance of *Ikhlaas*

- The *Basmalah*

Unit 5

The Significance of *Ikhlaas*

Word Bank

forbidden
virtue
intercession

Understanding the significance of *Ikhlaas*

- *Ikhlaas* is the basis of worship. Allah ﷻ will not accept any worship that is not done only for Him. If worship is done for anyone other than Allah ﷻ, then it will not be accepted.

- Actions that are done with a sincere intention and for the sake of Allah ﷻ will be rewarded by Allah ﷻ.

- If the intention for any act is to please Allah ﷻ and follow the *Sunnah*, it will be a virtuous act. But if the intention is to worship or please others or to show off, the act will have no *virtue*.

- Acts of worship and other good deeds must be based on knowledge and *ikhlaas*. *Ikhlaas* comes from the heart.

- Those who do good deeds and fulfill their religious duties with pure and clean intentions will be rewarded by Allah ﷻ.

A man came to the Prophet ﷺ, and asked, "What is the position of a man who has gone to battle wanting to be paid and be talked of for it." The Prophet ﷺ replied, "He has nothing." He then said, "Indeed Allah ﷻ accepts nothing except what was done with ikhlaas for His sake."

(Al-Bukhaari)

The Messenger of Allah ﷺ said, "If anybody comes on the Day of Resurrection who has said: 'Laa ilaaha illallaah, sincerely, with the intention to win Allah's ﷻ Pleasure, Allah ﷻ will make the Hell-Fire forbidden for him."

(Al-Bukhaari)

> **The Prophet ﷺ said,** *"The happiest people to get my intercession (asking Allah ﷻ for them not to be punished) are those who said, 'Laa ilaaha illa-llaah' with ikhlaas from their hearts or themselves."*
>
> (Al-Bukhaari)

1- **Which** of these sentences are true and which are false:

☐ a) A Muslim should do all acts of worship only for the sake of Allah ﷻ.

☐ b) If people worship others besides Allah ﷻ they will be rewarded by Allah ﷻ.

☐ c) Acts of worship do not require knowledge

☐ d) If the intention is for the sake of Allah ﷻ and according to the *Sunnah* of the Prophet Muhammad ﷺ, the act will be full of virtue.

☐ e) To have intentions to worship others and to show off will have no virtue.

2- **Which** two things are needed for acts of worship and good actions?

....

....

....

....

....

Activity 1

The following form lists a number of acts of worship, and a space for additional good deeds.

Complete the form by writing the following next to each of the listed deeds:

Write down the appropriate letter only.

a - Because your parents promised you something.

b - Because you wanted to show your friends or family.

c - Because your parents told you to do it.

d - Because you had to do it.

e - Because you knew that Allah ﷻ would be pleased if you did it.

Remember, everything you do should be for the pleasure of Allah ﷻ.
Be honest, it is only for your benefit.
Show the form to your parents and discuss ways in which you can improve yourself.

Day/Date	Fajr	Dhuhur	'Asr	Maghrib	Ishaa'	Qur'aan Recitation	Other Good Deeds (List each deed in) columns below)				
Day Before											
Yesterday											
Today											
Tomorrow											
After Day											

Activity 2

In your groups read the three *ahaadeeth* that appear in your text.
Discuss what you can learn from these *ahaadeeth*.
Write down the main points of your discussion and present it to your teacher in the form of an assignment.

Word Bank

niyyah
according to
pleasure
migration

Understanding the important position of *ikhlaas*

- Keeping one's *niyyah* pure is an important part of Islam. A correct *niyyah* is important for a Muslim's acts of worship and other good deeds to be accepted. It is also important for getting rewards for one's deeds.

- Allah ﷻ tells us that everything we do should be only for His pleasure.

Ikhlaas

Incorrect intention

"*Say, 'Indeed my prayer, my rites of sacrifice, my living and my dying are for Allah, Lord of the worlds.*"

(Soorah al-An'aam: 162)

The Prophet ﷺ said:

"*Surely actions are rewarded according to intentions, and every person shall receive what he has intended. So whosoever migrates to [please] Allah ﷻ and His Messenger ﷺ, his reward shall be for migration to Allah ﷻ and His Messenger ﷺ; and whosoever migrates for a reason of the world or to marry a woman, his reward will be for whatever he has migrated.*"

(Al-Bukhaari)

- In this *hadeeth*, the Prophet ﷺ tells us that an act will be judged and rewarded according to the person's *niyyah*.
  - If the intention is with *ikhlaas* (for Allah ﷻ alone), he will be rewarded accordingly.

- If the intention is for some other purpose the act will be looked at accordingly.
- If the intention is good and according to the Sunnah, then the act will be good.
- If the intention is bad, the act will be bad.

Since acts are judged by their intentions, many daily acts could become worship if their intention is to please Allah ﷻ.
Some examples are:

- Khadeejah goes to sleep early at night. She has the *niyyah* that she sleeps early so that she can rest and then wake fresh for the *Fajr* prayer. Her sleeping becomes an act of worship.

- Yoosuf is walking in the street. He sees an old woman struggling with some bags. He decides to help her and his *niyyah* is to seek reward from Allah ﷻ and to let the old woman see the good actions of a Muslim. This too becomes an act of worship.

Exercises

1- Briefly explain how important it is to have the correct intention in Islam.

The intention has to be important So you can have good deeds. and the intetion will be for the sake of Allah.

2- Fill in the blank spaces:

"Say, 'Indeed my *prayer*....., my rites of sacrifice, my ...*living*. and my dying are for ..*Allah*...., Lord of the worlds."

"Surely ..*actions* are rewarded according to their ...*intentions*, and every person shall receive what he has intended."

Activity 1

The **words** listed in the box below are hidden in the grid. **Find** and circle them.

action	worship
ikhlaas	reward
effort	Islam
	niyyah

s	w	o	r	s	h	i	p	c
g	r	k	o	n	e	q	l	h
s	s	w	e	z	f	x	t	i
i	l	l	g	n	f	b	n	k
q	a	c	t	i	o	n	o	h
j	m	m	k	y	r	r	f	l
y	p	c	h	y	t	d	a	a
u	r	e	w	a	r	d	v	a
d	m	i	f	h	p	e	j	s

Activity 2

Your teacher will divide you into groups of three.

a) In your lesson text you will find two examples of instances where daily acts can become worship simply by changing the intention for them. In your groups:
- Find those examples.
- Try to list three more examples from your daily activities.

b) There is a *hadeeth* in your lesson text. This *hadeeth* clearly explains the importance of *ikhlaas*.
- Find the *hadeeth*.
- Discuss its meaning and summarize it in three points.
- Memorize the first part of the *hadeeth* in Arabic and English.

Word Bank

basmalah

After seeking refuge in Allah ﷻ, Muslims say the basmalah.

- Reciting '*bismillaah*' (in the name of Allah ﷻ) is known as the *basmalah* and it is recommended before performing any action. The Messenger of Allah ﷺ used to begin every action with the *basmalah*.

- Before reading the *Qur'aan* Muslims should say, '**Bismillaahir-Rahmaanir-Raheem.**' It is necessary to read the *basmalah* at the beginning of each *soorah* except for *Soorah at-Tawbah*.

بِسْمِ اللهِ الرَّحْمٰنِ الرَّحِيمِ

- Muslims say the *basmalah*, to seek blessings for the action they are about to begin.

- After Muslims seek refuge and protection in Allah ﷻ, they then say, "***Bismillaahir-Rahmaanir-Raheem.***"

- It means: 'In the name of Allah ﷻ, the Entirely Merciful, the Especially Merciful.'

- ***Ar-Rahmaan*** and ***Ar-Raheem*** are two of Allah's ﷻ names that cannot be given to others. ***Ar-Rahmaan*** means that Allah ﷻ is the One Who has great mercy. ***Ar-Raheem*** means that He is the One Who treats others with mercy.

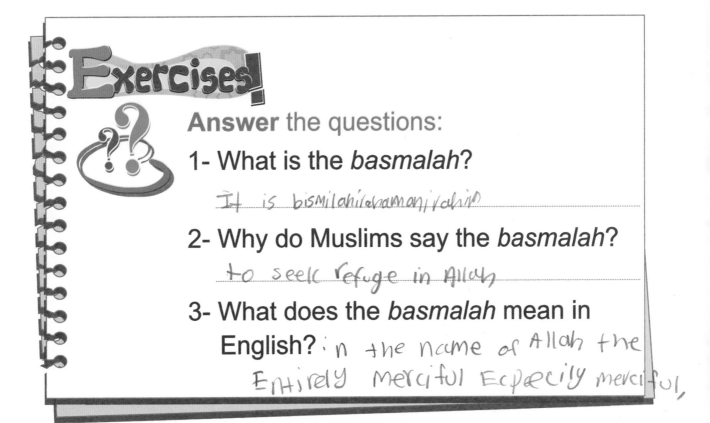

Exercises!

Answer the questions:

1- What is the *basmalah*?

It is bismilahirahamanjrahim

2- Why do Muslims say the *basmalah*?

to seek refuge in Allah

3- What does the *basmalah* mean in English? in the name of Allah the Entirely merciful Ecpecily merciful,

Activity 1

 **Listen** and Read!

أعوذ بالله من الشَّيطان الرَّجيم

بسم الله الرَّحمن الرَّحيم

Activity 2

What are '*ar*-Rahmaan' and '*ar*-Raheem'?
What do they mean?

- Ar-rahman means "The beneficent"
- ar-Raheem means "The merciful"

Unit 6

- *Ihsaan:* Review

- *Rabb* and *Ikhlaas:* Review

- Etiquettes of Reading the *Qur'aan:* Review

Ihsaan: Review

Do *Ihsaan*:
- In *'ibaadah*
- In daily life
  • At home,
  • At school or at work,
  • With parents or family,
  • With friends,
  • With strangers,
  • Travelers,
  • The poor,
  • The orphan,
  • The teacher,
  • The employee.

Show *Ihsaan* to:
• The rich and the poor,
• The young and the old,
• Good and bad people,
• Muslims and non-Muslims.

4 *Ihsaan* **at all Times**

Ihsaan

3 **Merits**

Allah ﷻ **rewards Muslims for all their good actions.**

The various merits of *Ihsaan* are:
• The *muhsin* will receive reward from Allah ﷻ
• Allah ﷻ is with those who do *Ihsaan*
• The *muhsin* is close to Allah's ﷻ mercy
• *Ihsaan* creates love for Allah ﷻ
• *Ihsaan* develops *taqwaa*
• *Ihsaan* creates love and unity.

To worship Allah ﷻ as if a person sees Allah ﷻ.
If he cannot reach this level, then he should know that Allah ﷻ is watching him,

- To act with goodness
- To have a kind way
- To do things perfectly

Such a person will :

- Do no wrong
- Not harm anybody
- Act with goodness
- Try his best in every deed

1 Meaning

A person who has *Ihsaan* is called a *muhsin*

Three Levels of *deen* (religion):
- *Islam*
- *Iman*
- *Ihsaan*

Ihsaan is the highest of the three. Allah ﷻ commands Muslims, in the *Qur'aan*, to act with *Ihsaan*.

2 Status and Importance

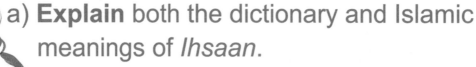

a) **Explain** both the dictionary and Islamic meanings of *Ihsaan*.

Ihsan means doing something in the best possible way it also means doing good to others.

b) **State** some benefits of *Ihsaan*.

- It develops taqwa in a muslim
- It keeps people sincer
- It improves the conditions of the society.

c) **Fill** in the blank spaces.

Ihsaan is the highest level of the .....deen.... levels of the religion. *Ihsaan* is higher than .....Iman.. and ...Islam.. The quality of *Ihsaan* is of great importance when engaging in any ...ibaabah.. of Allah ﷻ.

A person that has *Ihsaan* is known as a ..muhsin

A *muhsin* will be aware that Allah ﷻ is watching him/her whether at ..night... or during the day and whether in ..Secrete...... or in public.

Activity 1

- **Your** teacher will divide you into six groups. Each group will be given a topic, colored pencils, markers, crayons, and two large poster sheets.

- **You** will be required to:
  - Discuss the information on your topic.
  - Summarize the information on your topic.
  - Design a poster on your section.

- **You** are not allowed to use any other materials except those given to you by your teacher.

  The six topics are:
  - Definition of *Ihsaan*.
  - A person who does *Ihsaan* will act in the proper manner.
  - *Ihsaan* has a high status.
  - The merits of *Ihsaan*.
  - Ihsaan in worship.
  - How should *Ihsaan* be shown to others?

- **You** may reword the title.

Activity 2

In groups of three discuss ways in which:
- You can remind yourselves that Allah ﷻ is watching you all the time
- You can have *Ihsaan* in *'ibaadah*
  On your own, write two short paragraphs explaining these points.

Rabb and *Ikhlaas*
Review

Meaning

Worship
Rule   Create
Own   Provide
Control

Rabb

Signs
Recognizing the Lordship of the *Rabb* through His signs.

Signs
Recognizing the *Rabb* through His beautiful creations.

Ikhlaas

Meaning
- To be clean
- Pure Intention
- To do something only for the pleasure of Allah ﷻ.

Significance
If an act is done with *ikhlaas*, then there will be a reward.

Importance
Deeds are judged according to their intentions

1- **Explain** the meaning of *Rabb*.

Rabb means Allah because Allah means Rabb so rubb means Allah.

2- **Which** of these sentences are true and which are false ✖?

☒ a) *Ikhlaas* is to do an act for others together with Allah ﷻ.

☑ b) If the intention of an act is for the sake of Allah ﷻ, the act will be full of virtue.

☑ c) Allah ﷻ has the power to do anything that befits Him.

3- **Muslims** should stay away from every forbidden thing, do every type of good and kind action, and fulfil everyone's rights. This is what Allah ﷻ wants them to do. It should be for no other reason.

What is being described here?

Place the following words and phrases under the correct headings listed below.

(Worship) (Provide) (Intention)

(Own) (Clean)

(Create) (Pure) (Rule)

For the pleasure of Allah ﷻ,
Recognize the Creator through His creation
Deeds are judged according to intentions,
Know the Creator through His acts.

Rabb	*Ikhlaas*
Create	Pure
Worship	Intention
porvide	clean
rule	own

Activity 2

1- These are the first three words of an important *hadeeth*:

> *Innamal 'a'maalu binniyyaat*
>
> "إنمَا الأعمال بالنِّيَات"

Read it and remember what each word means. **Read** the words correctly and the teacher will help. Also try to remember the meanings.

2- Write down the meaning of the *hadeeth*.

This hadeeth means that Deed are based on intention. if your inteecton are good to do good Allah will reward you with good deeds.

Unit 6
Lesson 3
Etiquettes of Reading the *Qur'aan*: Review

Word Bank

etiquette

What are the etiquettes of reading the *Qur'aan*?

- Before Muslims touch the *Qur'aan* it is necessary to have *wudoo'*. The recitation of the *Qur'aan* is an *'ibaadah* (worship), and is the best form of *dhikr*.

- Muslims should use a *siwaak* before they read the *Qur'aan*. The Messenger of Allah ﷺ said,

"*The siwaak is a way to clean the mouth and please the Lord.*"

(Al-Bukhaari and Ahmad).

- When Muslims read the *Qur'aan* and use a *siwaak*, they will receive great rewards from Allah ﷻ.

- When Muslims recite the *Qur'aan*, they must recite with a melodious voice that is pleasing to hear and helps them memorize the *Qur'aan*. Prophet Muhammad ﷺ said, "Whoever does not beautify the *Qur'aan* (recite it melodiously) is not of us." (Al-Bukhaari)

- Allah ﷻ instructs Muslims to seek refuge from the rejected enemy *Shaytaan*, before reciting the *Qur'aan*.

Allah ﷻ says,

"So when you recite the Qur'aan , (first) seek refuge in Allah from Satan, the expelled (from his mercy)"

(*Soorah al-An'aam:* 162)

- After Muslims seek refuge and protection in Allah ﷻ, they then say, '*Bismillaahir-Rahmaanir-Raheem.*'

Exercises

1- Which word is used to explain that Muslims begin everything with the Name of Allah ﷻ? How is it read in Arabic?

....

....

....

....

....

2- Which word explains the act of Muslims seeking Refuge and Protection in Allah ﷻ? How is it read in Arabic?

....

....

....

....

....

....

Activity 1

Make a list of the etiquettes of reading the *Qur'aan*.

Activity 2

Discuss the following.

a) **Why** should we respect the *Qur'aan*?

○ ....

....

○ ....

b) **In** our society people show respect to the *Qur'aan* by:

○ ....

....

○ ....

c) **Summarize** your discussion in four points which one of your group will present to the class before the end of class.

○ ....

....

○ ....

Unit 7

○ **The Prophet** ﷺ **in the Cave of *Hiraa'***

○ **The Beginning of Revelation**

○ ***Soorah al-Inshiqaaq:* The Splitting Asunder (Part 1)**

Unit 7

The Prophet ﷺ in the Cave of *Hiraa'*

Word Bank

tahannuth
environment
saweeq
reflect
seclude

To know about the Prophet's ﷺ worship in the Cave of *Hiraa'*.

- As a young man, the Prophet Muhammad ﷺ was very thoughtful. As he grew older, he spent a lot of his time alone, reflecting on the creation. He thought about the people around him and how they were doing many bad things such as worshipping idols.

- When he was 33 years old, he removed himself from the environment of *shirk* and disbelief. He *secluded* himself in the Cave, of *Hiraa'*. It was a very small cave, north of Makkah, three miles from the Ka'bah .

94

He took *saweeq* (a type of barley porridge) and water along with him. As time passed, the Prophet Muhammad ﷺ went there more often, especially during the last three years before he received revelation.

- ʻAaʻishah ﵣ described how the Prophet ﷺ behaved at the start of the revelation. ʻAaʻishah ﵣ said that he saw good dreams when he was asleep, and any dream he had came true. The Prophet ﷺ liked to be alone during this time and went alone to the Cave of *Hiraaʻ*. He performed *tahannuth* there for many nights before returning to his family. *Tahannuth* means devotion and worship.

1- **List** the ways in which Muslims know that the Prophet Muhammad ﷺ led a perfect life.

1- Thaghtfil
2- Blivied in Allah
4- Worked very hard

2- **How** did 'Aa'ishah ؓ describe the Prophet ﷺ at the start of the revelation?

View the phrophet behaved at the start of revilil-on Aisha said he saw good dreams. Any droam will come true wenever the phrophet dromed

Activity 1

a) **In** groups of three, write down as many words as possible that describe the character and personality of the Prophet ﷺ.

1. Thaghtfd	5. refefect
2. Kind	6. Seredule
3. Tahunnuth	7. hard working
4. enviroment	8. reuillient

b) **Fill** in the blank spaces.

When he was .... years old, he removed himself from the environment of .... and ....
One of the places he used to .... himself in was the cave of .... The cave was extremely small and about .... miles north of Makkah. He would take .... (a type of barley porridge) and water along with him. As time passed, Muhammad ﷺ would go there more often, especialy during the last .... years before he received revelation.

Activity 2

Your teacher will guide you through the following activity.

• Close your eyes.

• Imagine you are in a cave.

• Think about the creation of Allah ﷻ and how this shows the greatness of Allah ﷻ

• Continue doing this for about three to five minutes

• Open your eyes.

• Write down what you were thinking and hand it to your teacher.

The Beginning of Revelation

Word Bank

wahyi (revelation)
communicates
occasional
divine
sign
directly

What is revelation? How did the wahyi (revelation) begin?

Wahyi

Direct speech
Vision / dream
Through angel
heart

- Allah ﷻ communicates with His creation in different ways. The Messengers of Allah ﷺ were sent to call people to the worship of Allah ﷻ alone and Revelations were sent so that people would know how to worship Allah ﷻ properly.

- Allah ﷻ sent revelation down to the messengers directly, through;

1- True dreams and visions,

2- Direct speech,

3- The angel Jibreel السلام,

4- Revelation directly into the heart of the messenger.

- Communication with the messengers is known as *wahyi* (revelation). *Wahyi* would therefore be the communication from Allah ﷻ to one of His messengers, either directly or through an angel.

- During the period of the Prophet's ﷺ visits to the Cave of *Hiraa'*, he would occasionally have true dreams. These were dreams wherein he would see such things that would take place in the future.

- When the Prophet ﷺ turned forty, the signs of prophethood began to increase and appear regularly. He saw more true dreams. These were the first revelations received by Prophet Muhammad ﷺ. Receiving revelation through dreams continued for a period of six months. The Prophet Muhammad ibn 'Abdullaah ﷺ was the last Prophet and Messenger to receive revelation.

 1- **True** ✔ or false ✘ ?

☒ a) **Allah** ﷻ sends revelation to any person.

☒ b) **With** some messengers revelation comes through direct speech.

☒ c) The Prophet **Muhammad ibn 'Abdullaah** ﷺ was not the last messenger.

☒ d) **People** will continue to receive revelation after the Prophet Muhammad ﷺ.

2- Allah ﷻ communicates with messengers in four ways. Name them.

Wahyi

true Dreams & visions

Allah ﷻ communicates with messengers in four ways.

angels Jibreel

revelation to the heart

'Ali was typing out a grid search for his brother, 'Uthmaan. When he printed it out he found that some of the vowels (a, e, i, o, or u) did not print well. Try to solve this grid search and work out the missing vowels.

wahyi   cave   angel

prophet   pressed   signs   dream

a	d	c	i	l	o	q	r	s
p	w	a	h	y	i	f	o	a
r	v	n	u	k	i	a	n
d	r		a	m	l	t	d	g
a	b	n	s	p		j	c	e
n	j	r	p	s	x	l	m	l
g	p	u	g	m		z	f	o
	s		g	n	s	d	a	b
l		p	r	o	p	h		t

Activity 2

 **Put** the following statements in their **correct** order, according to that which took place first.
Simply write down the letter of the statement.

◯ (A. Some true dreams.)

◯ (B. The Prophet ﷺ turned 40 years old.)

◯ (C. Began to seclude himself.)

◯ (D. 6 months.)

◯ (E. The Prophet ﷺ turned 33 years old.)

◯ (F. Regular true dreams.)

◯ (G. Worshipped Allah ﷻ in the cave.)

Soorah al-Inshiqaaq: The Split Asunder (Part 1)

Word Bank

reckoning
book of deeds

This part of the *soorah* shows some events that will occur on the Day of Judgment.

Soorah al-Inshiqaaq

Bismillaahir-Rahmaanir-Raheem

1. When the sky has split [open]

2. And has listened [i.e., responded] to its Lord and was obligated [to do so]

3. And when the earth has been extended

4. And has cast out that with in it and relinquished [it]

5. And has listened [i.e., responded] to its Lord and was obligated [to do so] —

بِسۡمِ اللهِ الرَّحۡمٰنِ الرَّحِيۡمِ

إِذَا السَّمَآءُ انشَقَّتۡ ۝

وَأَذِنَتۡ لِرَبِّهَا وَحُقَّتۡ ۝

وَإِذَا الۡأَرۡضُ مُدَّتۡ ۝

وَأَلۡقَتۡ مَا فِيهَا وَتَخَلَّتۡ ۝

وَأَذِنَتۡ لِرَبِّهَا وَحُقَّتۡ ۝

6. O mankind, indeed you are laboring toward your Lord with [great] exertion and will meet it.

يَـٰٓأَيُّهَا ٱلۡإِنسَـٰنُ إِنَّكَ كَادِحٌ إِلَىٰ رَبِّكَ كَدۡحٗا فَمُلَـٰقِيهِ ٦

7. Then as for he who is given his record in his right hand,

فَأَمَّا مَنۡ أُوتِيَ كِتَـٰبَهُۥ بِيَمِينِهِۦ ٧

8. He will be judged with an easy account

فَسَوۡفَ يُحَاسَبُ حِسَابٗا يَسِيرٗا ٨

9. And return to his people in happiness.

وَيَنقَلِبُ إِلَىٰٓ أَهۡلِهِۦ مَسۡرُورٗا ٩

10. But as for he who is given his record behind his back,

وَأَمَّا مَنۡ أُوتِيَ كِتَـٰبَهُۥ وَرَآءَ ظَهۡرِهِۦ ١٠

11. He will cry out for destruction

فَسَوۡفَ يَدۡعُواْ ثُبُورٗا ١١

12. And [enter to] burn in a Blaze.

وَيَصۡلَىٰ سَعِيرًا ١٢

13. Indeed, he had [once] been among his people in happiness;

إِنَّهُۥ كَانَ فِىٓ أَهۡلِهِۦ مَسۡرُورًا ١٣

14. Indeed, he had thought he would never return [to Allah].

إِنَّهُۥ ظَنَّ أَن لَّن يَحُورَ ١٤

15. But yes! Indeed, his Lord was ever, of him, Seeing.

بَلَىٰٓ إِنَّ رَبَّهُۥ كَانَ بِهِۦ بَصِيرٗا ١٥

(سورة الإنشقاق: ١-١٥)

We learn from the soorah

1- On the Day of Judgment, the sky will split into two.

2- The earth will be made flat and everything inside it will be thrown out.

3- Everyone will return to Allah عَزَّوَجَلَّ.

4- Then the Reckoning will take place.

5- Whoever is given his Book of Deeds in his right hand will enter Paradise.

6- Whoever is given his book of deeds behind his back will enter the blazing Fire.

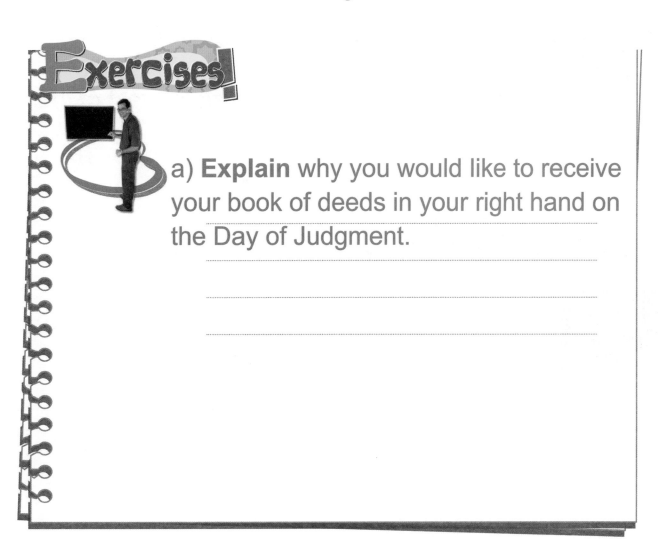

a) **Explain** why you would like to receive your book of deeds in your right hand on the Day of Judgment.

Activity 1

a) **Listen** to the teacher recite the *soorah* and repeat after him/her.

b) **Listen** to a recording of the *soorah* and repeat after each *aayah*.

Activity 2

a) **Recite** the third part of the *soorah* in a group.

b) **You** must recite the *soorah* to the teacher.

c) **One** student must recite and the rest of the students repeat after him/her.

Activity 3

Watch a video recording of a recitation of the *soorah* and try to imitate the reciter.

اقْرَأْ بِاسْمِ رَبِّكَ الَّذِي خَلَقَ

Unit 8

- The First Revelation

- Response of the Prophet ﷺ and Khadeejah رضي الله عنها

- *Soorah al-Inshiqaaq:* The Splitting Asunder (Part 2)

The First Revelation

Word Bank

frequent
Jibreel
stunning
embrace
tremble
miraculous

The revelation of the first few *aayaat of* Soorah al-'Alaq

- When the Prophet Muhammad ﷺ turned 40, he began to have frequent true dreams. This continued for a period of 6 months.

- In the month of Ramadaan, when the Prophet ﷺ was 40 years and six months old, Allah ﷻ blessed him with prophethood. Jibreel عليه السلام descended upon the command of Allah ﷻ, and the first few *aayaat* of the *Qur'aan* were revealed to the Prophet ﷺ.

Soorah al-'Alaq

Bismillaahir-Rahmaanir-Raheem

1. Recite in the name of your Lord who created –

اقْرَأْ بِٱسْمِ رَبِّكَ ٱلَّذِى خَلَقَ ۝

2. Created man from a clinging substance.

خَلَقَ ٱلْإِنسَـٰنَ مِنْ عَلَقٍ ۝

3. Recite, and your Lord is the most Generous –   ٱقۡرَأۡ وَرَبُّكَ ٱلۡأَكۡرَمُ ۝

4. Who taught by the pen –   ٱلَّذِى عَلَّمَ بِٱلۡقَلَمِ ۝

5. Taught man that which he knew not.   عَلَّمَ ٱلۡإِنسَـٰنَ مَا لَمۡ يَعۡلَمۡ ۝

(سورة العلق: ١-٥)

- The Prophet ﷺ was in the Cave thinking about the greatness of Allah ﷻ. Suddenly something appeared before him, which he had never seen before. Its appearance was stunning yet frightening. It was the Angel Jibreel عليه السلام.

  - Jibreel عليه السلام addressed the Prophet ﷺ and said, "Read!"

  - The Prophet ﷺ answered, "I cannot read".

  - Jibreel عليه السلام then took the Prophet ﷺ, embraced him firmly and again said, " Read!".

  - The Prophet ﷺ answered, "I cannot read."

  - Jibreel عليه السلام took hold of the Prophet ﷺ a second time, embraced him tightly, and again instructed him to read.

  - The Prophet ﷺ again answered, "I cannot read".

  - Jibreel عليه السلام embraced the Prophet ﷺ a third time.

  - Then he let go of him and recited to him the first few *aayaat* of *Soorah al-'Alaq*.

  - Trembling with fear, the Prophet ﷺ miraculously repeated the *aayaat* which Jibreel عليه السلام had recited to him.

The *Hadeeth* narrated by 'Aa'ishah ؓ about the first revelation

'Aa'ishah ؓ, the wife of the Prophet ﷺ narrates:

The commencement (of the Divine inspiration) to Allah's Apostle ﷺ, was in the form of true dreams in his sleep, for he never had a dream but it turned out to be true and clear as the bright daylight.

Then he began to like seclusion, so he used to go in seclusion in the Cave of *Hiraa'* where he used to worship Allah ﷻ continuously for many nights before going back to his family to take the necessary provision (of food) for the stay. He came back to (his wife) Khadeejah ؓ again to take his provision (of food) likewise, till one day he received the Guidance while he was in the Cave of *Hiraa'*.

An Angel came to him ﷺ and asked him to read, Allah's Apostle ﷺ replied, "«I do not know how to read,»" The Prophet ﷺ added, "«Then the Angel held me (forcibly) and pressed me so hard that I felt distressed. Then he released me and again pressed me for the second time till I felt distressed. He then released me and asked me to read, but again! I Replied. I do not know how to read. Thereupon he held me for the third time and pressed me till I got distressed, and then he released me and said:

"Recite, in the name of your Lord, who created - created man from a clinging substance, recite, and your Lord is most Generous, Who tauaght by the pen, taught man that which he knew not." (*Soorah al – 'Alaq*: 1-5)

(Al-Bukhaari)

Exercises!

Provide the answers to the following questions:

1- Which angel came to the Prophet Muhammad ﷺ with the revelation?

Angel jibreel Alahisallam.

2- In which month did the revelation of the first few *aayaat* of *Soorah al-'Alaq* take place?

In the month of Ramadan.

3- How old was the Prophet ﷺ at the time of revelation?

40 years and 6 months old.

4- Jibreel عليه السلام repeatedly instructed the Prophet ﷺ to do something. **What** was it?

He instructed the phrophet to "READ"

Activity 1

Your teacher will divide you into groups of four. Do the following:

- **Write** down the first five *aayaat* of the *Qur'aan* that were revealed. Write the Arabic as well as the English translation.

- **Practice** it in Arabic as a group.
- **Read** the English translation as a group.
- **Ask** your parents to help you memorize it at home.

Activity 2

Read through the *hadeeth* of 'Aa'ishah ﷺ then answer the following questions:

1- Who was 'Aa'ishah ﷺ?

2- What does the word 'seclude' mean?

3- What was the name of the angel who came to the Prophet ﷺ?

4- Can you name any other angels?

5- What is the name of the *soorah* in which the first *aayaat* appear?

6- How many times did Jibreel ﷺ press the Prophet ﷺ?

7- What did he ask the Prophet ﷺ to do?

8- Why did the Prophet ﷺ say, "I cannot read?"

9- In which book of *hadeeth* can you find this *hadeeth*?

Response of the Prophet ﷺ and Khadeejah رضي الله عنها

Word Bank

severe tremble
trudge
kith and kin
destitute
gospel /hebrew

What was the effect of the wahyi?

- The effect of the revelation of the first *aayaat* was so severe on the Prophet ﷺ that he began tremble His heart was beating strongly and his body shook with fear. In this condition he descended from the cave down the mountain and trudged the three miles back to the home of Khadeejah رضي الله عنها. 'Aa'ishah رضي الله عنها described this incident very clearly.

She says:

«Then Allah's Apostle ﷺ returned with the Inspiration and with his heart beating severely. Then he went to Khadeejah bint Khuwaylid ﴿ and said, «Cover me! «She covered him ﷺ till his fear subsided and after that he told her everything that had happened.»

● He then said ﷺ, «I fear that something may happen to me.» Khadeejah ﴿ replied, «Never! By Allah ﷻ, Allah ﷻ will never disgrace you. You keep good relations with your kith and kin, help the poor and the destitute, serve your guests generously and assist the deserving, calamity-afflicted ones.»

Khadeejah ﴿ then accompanied him to her cousin Waraqah ibn Nawfal (ibn Asad ibn Abdul Uzza), who, during the Pre-Islamic Period became a Christian and

used to write from the Gospel in Hebrew. He was an old man and had lost his eyesight.

- Khadeejah ؏ said to Waraqah, «Listen to the story of your nephew, O my cousin! Waraqah asked, «O my nephew! What have you seen?»

- Allah's Apostle ﷺ described whatever he had seen.

- Waraqah said, «This is the same one who keeps the secrets (Angel Jibreel ؏) whom Allah ﷻ had sent to Moosaa ؏. I wish I were young and could live up to the time when your people would drive you out.»

- Allah's Apostle ﷺ asked, «Will they drive me out?»

- Waraqah replied in the affirmative and said, «Anyone (man) who came with something similar to what you have brought was treated with hostility: and if I should remain alive till the day when you will be turned out then I would support you strongly.»

- But after a few days Waraqah died and the Divine Inspiration was also paused for a while..»

(Al-Bukhaari)

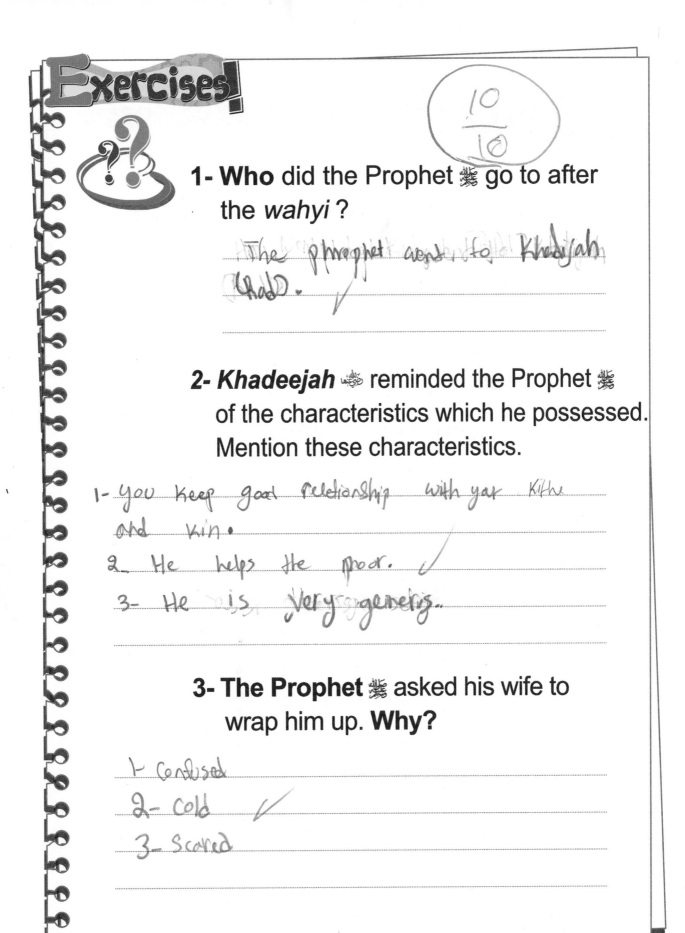

Exercises

1- Who did the Prophet ﷺ go to after the *wahyi* ?

The phrophet went fo Khadijah Khad.

2- Khadeejah ؓ reminded the Prophet ﷺ of the characteristics which he possessed. Mention these characteristics.

1- *you keep good relationship with your kithe and kin.*
2 *He helps the poor.*
3- *He is very generis.*

3- The Prophet ﷺ asked his wife to wrap him up. **Why?**

1- *Confused*
2- *Cold*
3- *Scared*

Aadam made a word search from this lesson. **His** older sister Maryam helped him type it on the computer.

To make it challenging she got him to write one of the words spelt backwards. Try to find all eight words:

wahyi	**prophet**	**voice**	**sky**
angel	**cover**	**wrap**	**fear**

```
E   G   R   E   V   O   C   I   B
M   W   R   W   X   U   A   P   K
U   B   A   G   S   I   N   R   H
V   M   E   H   K   R   G   O   C
O   Q   F   A   Y   Z   E   P   W
W   Q   L   N   Z   I   L   H   Y
D   R   H   V   O   I   C   E   L
M   F   A   F   K   J   Y   T   V
A   P   E   P   D   A   T   O   C
```

Activity 2

In groups of four do the following:

- Read through the *hadeeth* of 'Aa'ishah .

- Summarize it.

- Choose keywords for each of the main points.

- At home, write the definition and explanation of each of the keywords.

- Submit this to your teacher.

اقْرَأْ بِاسْمِ رَبِّكَ الَّذِي خَلَقَ

Unit 8

Lesson 3

Soorah al-Inshiqaaq:
The Splitting Asunder (Part 2)

Word Bank

prostrate

This part of the *soorah* shows how the disbelievers rejected the Oneness of Allah ﷻ

Soorah al-Inshiqaaq

Bismillaahir-Rahmaanir-Raheem

فَلَا أُقْسِمُ بِٱلشَّفَقِ ﴿١٦﴾

16. So I swear by the twilight glow

وَٱلَّيْلِ وَمَا وَسَقَ ﴿١٧﴾

17. And [by] the night and what it envelops

وَٱلْقَمَرِ إِذَا ٱتَّسَقَ ﴿١٨﴾

18. And [by] the moon when it becomes full

لَتَرْكَبُنَّ طَبَقًا عَن طَبَقٍ ﴿١٩﴾

19. [That] you will surely embark upon [i.e., experience] state after state.

فَمَا لَهُمْ لَا يُؤْمِنُونَ ﴿٢٠﴾

20. So what is [the matter] with them [that] they do not believe,

وَإِذَا قُرِئَ عَلَيْهِمُ ٱلْقُرْءَانُ لَا يَسْجُدُونَ ۩ ﴿٢١﴾

21. And when the Qur'aan is recited to them, they do not prostrate [to Allah]?

بَلِ ٱلَّذِينَ كَفَرُوا۟ يُكَذِّبُونَ ﴿٢٢﴾

22. But those who have disbelieved deny,

وَٱللَّهُ أَعْلَمُ بِمَا يُوعُونَ ﴿٢٣﴾

23. And Allah is most knowing of what they keep within themselves.

فَبَشِّرْهُم بِعَذَابٍ أَلِيمٍ ﴿٢٤﴾

24. So give them tidings of a painful punishment,

إِلَّا ٱلَّذِينَ ءَامَنُوا۟ وَعَمِلُوا۟ ٱلصَّٰلِحَٰتِ

25. Except for those who believe and do righteous deeds. For them is a reward uninterrupted.

لَهُمْ أَجْرٌ غَيْرُ مَمْنُونٍ ﴿٢٥﴾

(سورة الإنشقاق: ١٦-٢٥)

1- The disbelievers do not prostrate to Allah ﷻ when the *Qur'aan* is recited.

2- It is normal for a disbeliever to reject the truth.

3- Allah ﷻ knows exactly what they hide in their hearts.

4- Allah ﷻ has prepared a painful punishment for the disbelievers.

Exercises!

Why does Allah ﷻ warn the disbelievers about a painful punishment in verse 24?

Activity 1

a) **Listen** to the teacher recite the *soorah* and repeat after him/her.

b) **Listen** to a recording of the *soorah* and repeat after each *aayah*.

Activity 2

a) **Recite** this part of the *soorah* in a group.

b) **Recite** the *soorah* to the teacher.

c) **One** student will recite and the rest of the students repeat after him/her.

Activity 3

Watch a video recording of a recitation of the *soorah* and try to imitate the reciter.

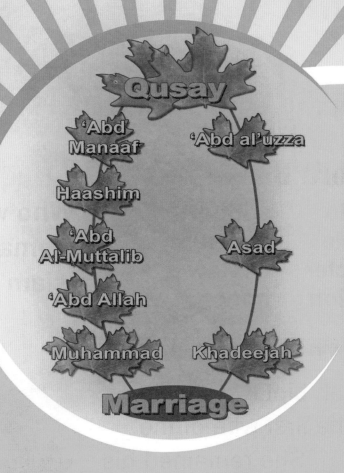

Qusay

'Abd Manaaf   'Abd al'uzza

Haashim

'Abd Al-Muttalib   Asad

'Abd Allah

Muhammad   Khadeejah

Marriage

Unit 9

○ **The First Woman to Accept Islam**

○ **The First Man to Accept Islam**

○ *Soorah al-Mutaffifeen:* **Those who Give Incorrect Weight or Measure (Part 1)**

The First Woman to Accept Islam

Word Bank

tremble	support
console	reassure
character	bestow
occasion	honor

Who was the first woman to accept Islam?

- Khadeejah bint Khuwaylid رضي الله عنها was the first wife of the Prophet ﷺ. She remained his only wife for her lifetime.

- She married the Prophet ﷺ when he was 25 years old,[1] and she was 40 at the time. She was very wealthy and she asked the Prophet ﷺ to do some business on her behalf. She was impressed by his character and qualities and felt that he would be the ideal husband.

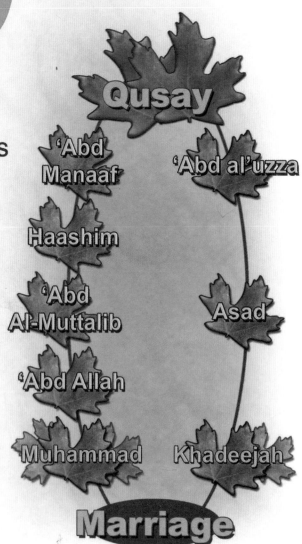

1- Al Mubarakpuri, S.R, The Sealed Nectar, Darussalam, 2002, Pg. 78, 79.

- Throughout their marriage, she remained the perfect wife. She was the mother of six of the Prophet's ﷺ seven children. She also took good care of her family. When the Prophet ﷺ began to seclude himself in the Cave of *Hiraa'*, for long periods, she never objected to that. She used to prepare food for him. Thus, Khadeejah ﵂ supported the Prophet ﷺ in everything he did.

- When the Prophet ﷺ received the first revelation, he was visibly shaken and returned home sweating and trembling. Khadeejah ﵂ consoled him, covered him with a blanket and helped him calm down. When he told her what had happened and that he feared for his life, Khadeejah ﵂ reassured him.

- She also praised his excellent character and told him that Allah ﷻ would never allow any harm to come to him.

- Khadeejah ﵂ believed in the character of the Prophet ﷺ. After listening to the Prophet ﷺ, she took him to her cousin Waraqah Ibn Nawfal. Waraqah affirmed that what happened to Muhammad ﷺ was the beginning of Prophethood ﷺ.

- Khadeejah ﵂ accepted Islam and made her declaration of faith. At that stage, Khadeejah ﵂ was the first woman to accept Islam. Khadeejah ﵂ was greatly honored because of this.

> **The Prophet ﷺ said,**
> "The best woman of her time was Maryam and
> And the best woman of her time was Khadeejah رضي الله عنها."
>
> *(Al-Bukhaari)*

Answer the questions:

1- **Name** the grandfather of both the Prophet ﷺ and Khadeejah رضي الله عنها.

   Abdul Manaf, Abd ul uzaa.

2- **How** many children did the Prophet ﷺ and Khadeejah رضي الله عنها have.

   The phophet and Khadijah had
   7 children of the phophet
   6 children of Khadijah.

3- **Who** was the first woman to accept Islam?

Khadijah (RA) (~~Khadijah (RA)~~) was the first women to exept Islam.

4- **How** soon after the Prophet ﷺ received the first revelation did Khadeejah ﷺ accept Islam?

Imjdienlty after the phrophet told her about the cave of hira.

5- **What** was Khadeejah's ﷺ cousin's name?

Khadijah's cosion name is waraqah ibn Nawfal

Activity 1

Your teacher will divide you into groups of three.

He/she will also provide you with some research material.

In groups, do the following:

- **Read** the material given to you.

- **Make** a note of all the points that show Khadeejah's ﷺ dedication to the Prophet ﷺ.

- **Draw up** a poster using these points.

- **The** best poster will go on the school notice board.

Activity 2

At home, write a paragraph, on any two of the following topics.
Each paragraph should be at least 100 words long.

Topics:

- Khadeejah ﷺ was a great woman.

- Khadeejah ﷺ was the first supporter of *da'wah* in Islam.

- Khadeejah ﷺ is a good role model for Muslim women.

The First Man to Accept Islam

Word Bank

clan
youth
khaleel
dedicated

Who was the first man to accept Islam?

- Aboo Bakr ؓ was a highly respected man of his time in and around Makkah. He was responsible for making decisions on things for the entire Quraysh. He was the chief of his clan.

- Aboo Bakr ؓ was known for his humility and kindness. He always helped the poor and was known for his generosity. He stayed away from wrong actions and never drank wine.

- In their youth, Aboo Bakr ؓ and the Prophet ﷺ were close friends. Aboo Bakr ؓ probably knew the Prophet ﷺ better than any other man. He also understood the character and personality of the Prophet ﷺ .

- After the Prophet ﷺ received the first revelation, he met with Aboo Bakr ؓ. The Prophet ﷺ informed Aboo Bakr ؓ of the incident in the Cave of *Hiraa'* and that Allah ﷻ had chosen him (Muhammad) ﷺ as His Messenger.

- Aboo Bakr ؓ asked no questions and he had no issues to discuss. As soon as the Prophet ﷺ informed him, Aboo Bakr ؓ accepted the statement of the Prophet ﷺ and declared his faith in Allah ﷻ and the prophethood of Muhammad ﷺ . Aboo Bakr ؓ was the first man to accept Islam.

- Aboo Bakr ؓ dedicated his wealth and life for the cause of Islam.

The Prophet ﷺ praised him a lot. The Prophet ﷺ said, "The person who supported me the most with both his friendship and wealth is Aboo Bakr . If I were to take anyone as khaleel (most intimate companion), other than my Rabb, I would have taken Aboo Bakr for a khaleel. However, Islamic brotherhood and love is present. Let every gate of the mosque be closed except that of Aboo Bakr ."

(Al-Bukhaari)

Exercises!

1- Mention three aspects of Aboo Bakr's ﷺ character.

....

....

....

....

2- How did Aboo Bakr ﷺ support Islam and help the Muslims?

....

....

....

Activity 1

Your teacher will divide you into groups of three.

He/she will also provide you with some research material.

In groups, do the following:

- **Read** the material given to you.

- **Make** a note of all the points that show Aboo Bakr's ﷛ closeness to the Prophet ﷺ.

- **Draw up** a poster using these points.

- **The** best poster will go on the school notice board.

Activity 2 ✓

At home, write a paragraph, on any two of the following three topics.
Each paragraph should be at least 100 ~~50~~ words .

Topics:

- The character of Aboo Bakr ﷺ

- Merits of Aboo Bakr ﷺ

- Aboo Bakr ﷺ was the first man to accept Islam ✓

- Abu Bakar was a very kind man to the phrophet (saw). He was a very hiliy Respected man. He was known for his humility and kindness. He stayed away from wrong actions and never drank wine. Abu Bakar (RA) was a close friend to the prhophet (saw). Abu Bakar (RA) dedicated his wealth and life for the cause of islam.

Soorah al-Mutaffifeen: Those Who Give Incorrect Weight or Measure (Part 1)

Word Bank

measurement
weigh

This part of the *soorah* teaches man that loss and destruction will befall those who weigh incorrectly and give less to their customers.

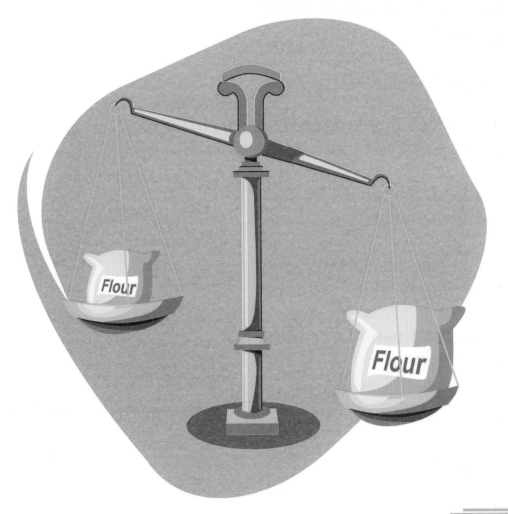

Flour

Flour

Soorah al-Mutaffifeen

Bismillaahir-Rahmnir-Raheem

وَيْلٌ لِّلْمُطَفِّفِينَ ۝

1. Woe to those who give less [than due], ←

ٱلَّذِينَ إِذَا ٱكْتَالُواْ عَلَى

2. Who, when they take a measure from
   people, take in full. ←

ٱلنَّاسِ يَسْتَوْفُونَ ۝

3. But if they give by measure or by
   weight to them, they cause loss. ←

وَإِذَا كَالُوهُمْ أَو وَّزَنُوهُمْ يُخْسِرُونَ ۝

4. Do they not think that they will
   be resurrected ←

أَلَا يَظُنُّ أُوْلَئِكَ أَنَّهُم مَّبْعُوثُونَ ۝

5. For a tremendous Day – ←

لِيَوْمٍ عَظِيمٍ ۝

6. The Day when mankind will stand
   before the Lord of the worlds? ←

يَوْمَ يَقُومُ ٱلنَّاسُ لِرَبِّ ٱلْعَالَمِينَ ۝

7. No! Indeed, the record of the
   wicked is in sijjeen. ←

كَلَّا إِنَّ كِتَابَ ٱلْفُجَّارِ لَفِي سِجِّينٍ ۝

8. And what can make you know
   what is *sijjeen*? ←

وَمَآ أَدْرَىكَ مَا سِجِّينٌ ۝

9. It is [their destination recorded in]
   a register inscribed. ←

كِتَابٌ مَّرْقُومٌ ۝

10. Woe, that Day, to the deniers,

وَيْلٌ يَوْمَئِذٍ لِّلْمُكَذِّبِينَ ﴿١٠﴾

11. Who deny the Day of Recompense.

ٱلَّذِينَ يُكَذِّبُونَ بِيَوْمِ ٱلدِّينِ ﴿١١﴾

12. And none deny it except every sinful transgressor.

وَمَا يُكَذِّبُ بِهِ إِلَّا كُلُّ مُعْتَدٍ أَثِيمٍ ﴿١٢﴾

إِذَا تُتْلَىٰ عَلَيْهِ ءَايَٰتُنَا

13. When Our verses are recited to him, he says, "Legends of the former peoples."

قَالَ أَسَٰطِيرُ ٱلْأَوَّلِينَ ﴿١٣﴾

كَلَّا ۖ بَلْ رَانَ عَلَىٰ قُلُوبِهِم

مَّا كَانُوا۟ يَكْسِبُونَ ﴿١٤﴾

14. No! Rather, the stain has covered their hearts of that which they were earning.

كَلَّا إِنَّهُمْ عَن رَّبِّهِمْ يَوْمَئِذٍ لَّمَحْجُوبُونَ ﴿١٥﴾

15. No! Indeed, from their Lord, that Day, they will be partitioned.

ثُمَّ إِنَّهُمْ لَصَالُوا۟ ٱلْجَحِيمِ ﴿١٦﴾

16. Then indeed, they will [enter and] burn in Hellfire.

ثُمَّ يُقَالُ هَٰذَا ٱلَّذِى كُنتُم بِهِ تُكَذِّبُونَ ﴿١٧﴾

17. Then it will be said [to them], "This is what you used to deny."

كَلَّا إِنَّ كِتَٰبَ ٱلْأَبْرَارِ لَفِى عِلِّيِّينَ ﴿١٨﴾

18. No! Indeed, the record of the righteous is in 'illiyyoon.

وَمَا أَدْرَىٰكَ مَا عِلِّيُّونَ ﴿١٩﴾

19. And what can make you know what is 'illiyyoon?

كِتَٰبٌ مَّرْقُومٌ ﴿٢٠﴾

20. It is [their destination recorded in] a register inscribed

(سورة المطففين: ١-٢٠)

We learn from the soorah

1- *Mutaffifeen* are those people who demand full measure when something is weighed for them.

2- When they weigh for others, they give less.

3- Allah ﷻ has promised loss and destruction to people who do this.

4- Their names are written in a book that they will be in *Sijjeen* after they die.

5- *Sijjeen* is a place underneath the seventh earth where evil people will be punished.

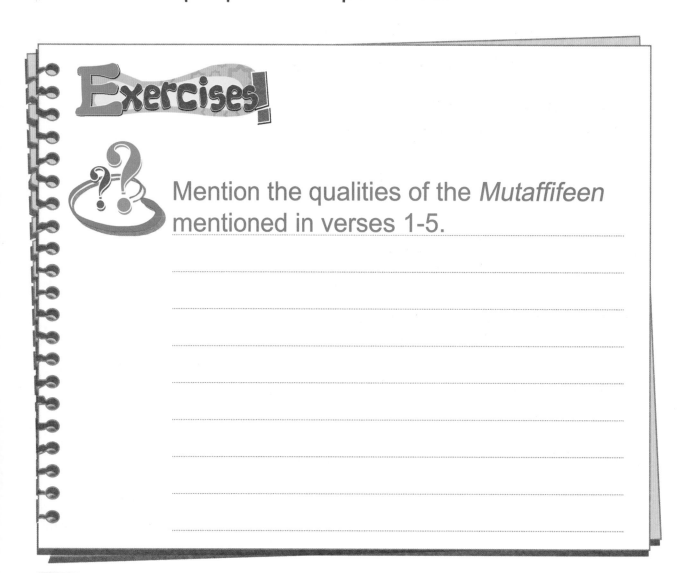

Exercises!

Mention the qualities of the *Mutaffifeen* mentioned in verses 1-5.

Activity 1

a) **Listen** to the teacher recite the *soorah* and repeat after him/her.

b) **Listen** to a recording of the *soorah* and repeat after each *aayah*.

Activity 2

a) **Recite** this part of the *soorah* in a group.

b) **Recite** the *soorah* to the teacher.

c) **One** student will recite and the rest of the students repeat after him/her.

Activity 3

Watch a video recording of a recitation of the *soorah* and try to imitate the reciter.

Unit 10

○ Review: *Wahyi (Revelation)*

○ Review: **First Muslims**

○ *Soorah al-Mutaffifeen :*
**Those Who Give Incorrect
Weight or Measure: (Part 2)**

Unit 10

اقرأ Review: *Wahyi (Revelation)*

Word Bank
character
seclusion
revelation

A review of lessons: 7.1, 7.2, 8.1, 8.2

Unit 7   Lesson 1

Worship in the Cave of *Hiraa*
- The Prophet ﷺ, a perfect example
- Excellent Character
- Stayed away from wrong actions
- Practice of Seclusion
- Cave of *Hiraa'*

Worship in the Cave of *Hiraa'*
- Think about wrongs
- Pain and Frustration at wrongs
- Ponder over creation
- Ponder on greatness of Allah ﷻ
- Realize the greatness of Allah ﷻ

Unit 7   Lesson 2

Revelation and Dreams
- Meaning of revelation
- Reason for revelation
- Who receives revelation
- Forms of revelation

Dreams as a form of revelation
- Prophet's ﷺ seclusion in cave
- Occasional dreams
- Prophet ﷺ turns 40 years old
- Regular true dreams begin
- True dreams continue for 6 months

Unit 8   Lesson 1

First Revelation
- The Prophet ﷺ turns 40 years old
- Regular true dreams 6 months
  - Month of Ramadaan arrives
  - Prophet ﷺ in Cave of *Hiraa'*
- Jibreel عليه السلام descends
- Incident with Jibreel عليه السلام
- First Revelation
- 5 *aayaat* of *Soorah al-'Alaq*

Unit 8   Lesson 2

Effect of Revelation
- Jibreel عليه السلام descends
- Incident with Jibreel عليه السلام
- Awesome event
- Prophet ﷺ fearful
  - Trembling and sweating; returns home
  - Khadeejah ﵂ covers Prophet ﷺ with blanket
  - Khadeejah ﵂ consoles and reassures him
- Meeting with Waraqah Ibn Nawfal
- Waraqah confirms prophethood from his knowledge

1- **Explain** the following words:

Wahyi	Seclusion

2- **Explain** who the following were :

Jibreel	Waraqah Ibn Nawfal

Activity 1

Your teacher will divide you into groups of four. **Your** teacher will also select a lesson for each group.

In your groups do the following:

- **Read** through the actual lesson under review.
- **Read** through the summary of the lesson.
- **Make** your own summary of the lesson.
- **One person** from your group will have to present the summary. (Every student should be prepared, since the teacher will select the presenters in each group.)

Activity 2

Entire sections from the summaries have been mixed up. Rearrange the summaries in such a way that the points are all in their correct boxes

---

Unit 7   Lesson 1

Worship in the Cave of Hiraa'
- The Prophet ﷺ is a perfect example
- Excellent character
- Stayed away from wrong actions
- Practice of Seclusion
- Cave of *Hiraa'*

Worship in the Cave of *Hiraa'*
- Think about wrongs
- Pain and frustration at wrongs
- Ponder over creation
- Ponder on greatness of Allah ﷻ
- Realize the greatness of Allah ﷻ

Unit 7   Lesson 2

Revelation and Dreams
- Meaning of revelation
- Reason for revelation
- Who receives revelation
- Forms of revelation

Dreams as a form of revelation
- Prophet's ﷺ seclusion in cave
- Occasional dreams
- Prophet ﷺ turns 40 years old
- Regular true dreams begin
- True dreams continue for 6 months

Unit 8   Lesson 1

First Revelation
- Prophet ﷺ turns 40 years old
- Regular true dreams 6 months
  - The Month of Ramadaan arrives
  - Prophet ﷺ in Cave of *Hiraa'*
- Jibreel عليه السلام descends
- Incident with Jibreel عليه السلام
- First Revelation
- 5 *aayaat* of *Soorah al-'Alaq*

Unit 8   Lesson 2

Effect of Revelation
- Jibreel عليه السلام descends
- Incident with Jibreel
- Awesome event
- Prophet ﷺ fearful
  - Trembling and sweating returns home
  - Khadeejah رضي الله عنها covers Prophet ﷺ with blanket
  - Kahdeejah رضي الله عنها consoles and reassures him
- Meeting with Waraqah Ibn Nawfal
- Waraqah confirms prophethood from his knowledge

Review: First Muslims

Word Bank
lineage
reassure
console
declaration
merit

To review lessons on the First Muslims

Unit 9 — Lesson 1

First Woman to Accept Islam

Khadeejah Bint Khuwaylid
- Lineage
- Wealthy woman
- Business dealings with the Prophet
- Impressed by his character
- Marriage to the Prophet
- Perfect wife
- 6 children
- Respected her husband
- Supported the Prophet in all his efforts
- Prophet shaken after 1st revelation
- Khadeejah consoles him
- Reassures him
- Gives glowing description of Prophet's character
- Meeting with Waraqah
- Knowledge of prophethood
- Declaration of faith
- The merits of Khadeejah

Unit 9 — Lesson 2

First Man to Accept Islam

Aboo Bakr
- Highly respected
- Judge amongst Quraysh regarding blood money
- Chief of clan
- Known for goodness
- Assisted the poor and needy
- Stayed away from evil
- Never drank wine
- Close friend of the Prophet from youth
- Knew Prophet well
- Prophet receives 1st revelation
- The Prophet spoke to Aboo Bakr
- Aboo Bakr informed about revelation and prophethood
- Aboo Bakr accepts Islam without questioning anything
- Merit of Aboo Bakr

1- **What** type of friend was Aboo Bakr ﷺ to the Prophet ﷺ ?

....

....

2- **Describe** some characteristics of Aboo Bakr ﷺ.

....

....

3- **Who** was the first woman to accept Islam and how was she related to the Prophet ﷺ?

....

....

4- **Mention** some characteristics of Khadeejah ﷺ.

....

....

5- **How** many children did the Prophet ﷺ and Khadeejah ﷺ have?

....

....

Activity 1

Your teacher will divide you into groups of four.

He/She will also select a lesson for each group.

In your groups do the following:

- **Read** through the actual lesson under review.
- **Read** through the summary of the lesson.
- **Make** your own summary of the lesson.
- **One** person from your group will have to present the summary. (Every student should be prepared, since the teacher will select the presenters in each group.)

Activity 2

Entire sections from the summaries have been mixed up.

Rearrange the summaries in such a way that the points are all in their correct boxes

---

Unit 9   Lesson 2

First Man to Accept Islam
Aboo Bakr ❁

- His Lineage
- Wealthy woman
- Business ❁ dealings with
- the Prophet ❁
- Impressed by his character
- Marriage to the Prophet ❁
- Perfect wife
- 6 children
- Respected her husband
- Supported the Prophet ❁ in all
- Close friend of the Prophet
- ❁ from youth
- Prophet ❁ shaken after first
- revelation
- Khadeejah ❁ consoles him
- Reassures him
- Knowledge of prophethood
- Declaration of faith
- Merits of Khadeejah ❁

Unit 9   Lesson 1

First Woman to Accept Islam
Khadeejah Bint Khuwaylid ❁

- Highly respected
- Judge amongst Quraysh regarding blood money
- Chief of clan
- Known for goodness
- Assisted the poor and needy
- Stayed away from evil
- practices
- Never drank wine
- Knew the Prophet ❁ well
- Gives glowing description of Prophet's ❁ character
- The Prophet ❁ receives the
- first revelation
- Meeting with Aboo Bakr ❁
- Aboo Bakr ❁ informed about revelation and prophethood
- Meeting with Waraqah
- Aboo Bakr ❁ accepts Islam without questioning anything
- Merits of Aboo Bakr ❁

151

Soorah al-Mutaffifeen
Those Who Give Incorrect Weight or Measure (Part 2)

Word Bank

seventh heaven

musk

This part of the *soorah* shows some of the luxuries that await those who will enter Paradise.

Soorah al-Mutaffifeen
Bismillaahir-Rahmaanir-Raheem

بِسۡمِ ٱللَّهِ ٱلرَّحۡمَٰنِ ٱلرَّحِيمِ

يَشۡهَدُهُ ٱلۡمُقَرَّبُونَ ﴿٢١﴾

21. Which is witnessed by those brought near [to Allah].

إِنَّ ٱلۡأَبۡرَارَ لَفِى نَعِيمٍ ﴿٢٢﴾

22. Indeed, the righteous will be in pleasure

عَلَى ٱلۡأَرَآئِكِ يَنظُرُونَ ﴿٢٣﴾

23. On adorned couches, observing.

تَعۡرِفُ فِى وُجُوهِهِمۡ نَضۡرَةَ ٱلنَّعِيمِ ﴿٢٤﴾

24. You will recognize in their faces the radiance of pleasure.

25. They will be given to drink [pure] wine [which was] sealed. ◄

يُسْقَوْنَ مِن رَّحِيقٍ مَّخْتُومٍ ٢٥

خِتَـٰمُهُۥ مِسْكٌ ۚ وَفِى ذَٰلِكَ فَلْيَتَنَافَسِ ٱلْمُتَنَـٰفِسُونَ ٢٦

26. The last of it is musk. So for this let the competitors compete. ◄

27. And its mixture is of *Tasneem*, ◄

وَمِزَاجُهُۥ مِن تَسْنِيمٍ ٢٧

28. A spring from which those near [to Allah] drink. ◄

عَيْنًا يَشْرَبُ بِهَا ٱلْمُقَرَّبُونَ ٢٨

إِنَّ ٱلَّذِينَ أَجْرَمُوا۟ كَانُوا۟ مِنَ ٱلَّذِينَ ءَامَنُوا۟ يَضْحَكُونَ ٢٩

29. Indeed, those who committed crimes used to laugh at those who believed. ◄

30. And when they passed by them, they would exchange derisive glances. ◄

وَإِذَا مَرُّوا۟ بِهِمْ يَتَغَامَزُونَ ٣٠

31. And when they returned to their people, they would return jesting. ◄

وَإِذَا ٱنقَلَبُوٓا۟ إِلَىٰٓ أَهْلِهِمُ ٱنقَلَبُوا۟ فَكِهِينَ ٣١

وَإِذَا رَأَوْهُمْ قَالُوٓا۟ إِنَّ هَـٰٓؤُلَآءِ لَضَآلُّونَ ٣٢

32. And when they saw them, they ◄ would say, "Indeed, those are truly lost."

33. But they had not been sent as guardians over them. ◄

وَمَآ أُرْسِلُوا۟ عَلَيْهِمْ حَـٰفِظِينَ ٣٣

فَٱلْيَوْمَ ٱلَّذِينَ ءَامَنُوا۟ مِنَ ٱلْكُفَّارِ يَضْحَكُونَ ٣٤

34. So Today those who ◄ believed are laughing at the disbelievers,

35. On adorned couches, observing. ◄

عَلَى ٱلْأَرَآئِكِ يَنظُرُونَ ٣٥

36. Have the disbelievers [not] been rewarded [this Day] for what they used to do?

هَلْ ثُوِّبَ ٱلْكُفَّارُ مَا كَانُوا۟ يَفْعَلُونَ ٣٦

(سورة المطففين: ٢١-٣٦)

We learn from the soorah

1- The names of those who will enter Paradise are written in a book which is in 'Illiyyoon.

2- 'Illiyyoon is a place high up in the seventh heaven.

3- Those in Paradise will drink pure wine with an aftertaste of musk.

4- They will sit on raised couches and look at each other.

5- They will laugh at the disbelievers as the disbelievers laughed at them in this world.

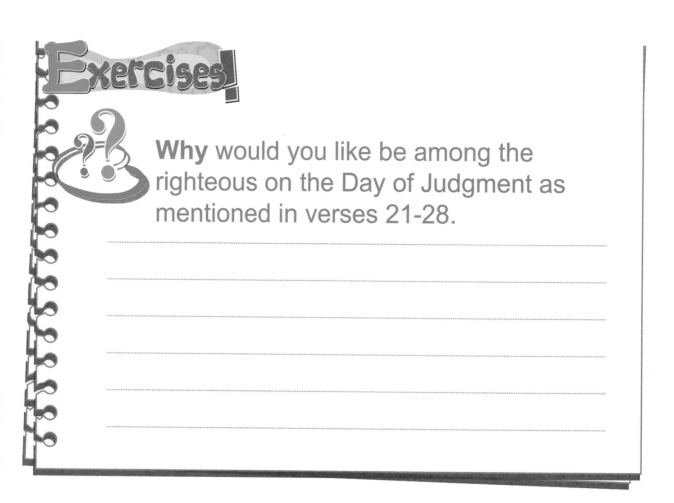

Why would you like be among the righteous on the Day of Judgment as mentioned in verses 21-28.

Activity 1

a) Listen to the teacher recite the *soorah* and repeat it after him.

b) Listen to a recording of the *soorah* and repeat after each *aayah*.

Activity 2

a) Recite this part of the *soorah* in a group.

b) Recite the *soorah* to the teacher.

c) One student will recite and the rest of the students repeat after him/her.

Activity 3

Watch a video recording of the recitation of the *soorah* and try to imitate the reciter.

Unit 11

- **The First Boy to Accept Islam**
- **Things that Break** *Wudoo'*
- **Review of** *Qur'aan* : *Soorah al-Mutaffifeen (Part 1&2) and Soorah al-Inshiqaaq (Parts 1&2)*

The First Boy to Accept Islam

Word Bank
hesitation
starve

'Ali Ibn Abee Taalib ﷺ is one of the foremost people in Islam.

- 'Ali Ibn Abee Taalib Ibn 'Abdul-Muttalib Ibn 'Abd Manaaf is a very important person in Islamic history. He is also known as Abul-Hasan and Aboo Turaab.

- 'Ali ﷺ was the cousin of Prophet Muhammad ﷺ and lived with him and Khadeejah ﷺ in their house. Once 'Ali ﷺ saw them praying in a way that he had never seen before and he asked about it. The Prophet Muhammad ﷺ told him that Allah ﷻ had sent him to

teach Islam to all people. He explained what Islam is and asked him to become a Muslim.

- 'Ali ؓ was hesitant and said that he would have to talk to his father Aboo Taalib first. The Prophet ﷺ told him to keep it a secret. 'Ali knew that the Prophet ﷺ was truthful and the following day he became a Muslim.

- 'Ali ؓ was twelve years old at the time and was the first boy to accept Islam. He asked the Prophet ﷺ to teach him how to pray so that they could all pray in the house together.

- 'Ali ؓ memorized the *aayaat* of the Qur'aan as soon as they were revealed to the Prophet ﷺ. When the Prophet ﷺ began calling people to Islam in public, more people became Muslims. Many times he would see people making fun of the Prophet ﷺ and he would stop them. 'Ali ؓ was very brave and strong.

- When Aboo Taalib and Khadeejah ؓ passed away, there was not much help for the Muslims in Makkah. 'Ali ؓ became an orphan and the Prophet ﷺ supported and looked after him.

- At the time, the Muslims were very weak and the Arab tribes wanted to kill them. The Prophet ﷺ allowed some of the first Muslims to leave to a safer country in Africa called Habashah. Aboo Bakr ؓ and 'Ali ؓ stayed in Arabia with the Prophet ﷺ and tried to teach people about Islam.

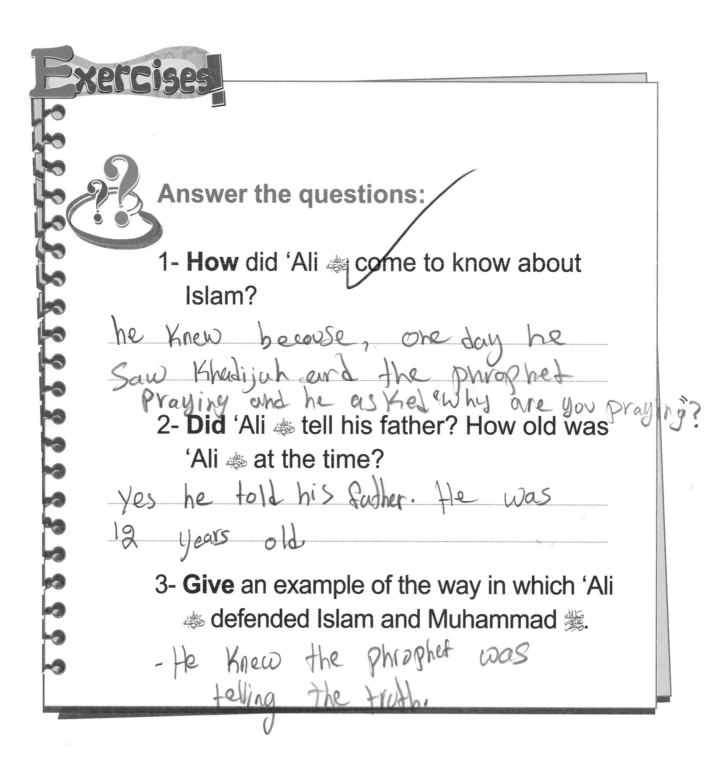

Exercises!

Answer the questions:

1- **How** did 'Ali ﷺ come to know about Islam?

he Knew because, one day he Saw Khadijah and the phrophet Praying and he asked "why are you praying"?

2- **Did** 'Ali ﷺ tell his father? How old was 'Ali ﷺ at the time?

Yes he told his father. He was 12 years old

3- **Give** an example of the way in which 'Ali ﷺ defended Islam and Muhammad ﷺ.

- He knew the phrophet was telling the truth.

16/16

1- 'Ali's ﷺ full name was

☑ a) Abul-Hasan 'Ali Ibn Abee Taalib Ibn 'Abdul-Muttallib Ibn 'Abd-Manaaf.

☐ b) Abul-Hasan 'Ali Ibn Abee Taalib Ibn 'Abdul-Muttallib Ibn Manaaf.

☐ c) Abul-Hasan 'Ali Ibn Abee Taalib Ibn Abee Lahab Ibn Al-Qurayshi.

2- 'Ali ﷺ was the

☐ a) brother of Muhammad ﷺ.

☐ b) uncle of Muhammad ﷺ.

☑ c) cousin of Muhammad ﷺ.

3- When 'Ali ﷺ became a Muslim he was

☐ a) 5 years old.

☐ b) 7 years old.

☑ c) 12 years old.

4- **When** 'Ali ﷺ saw people making fun of the Prophet ﷺ he would

☐ a) join along with them.

☐ b) get scared and run away.

☒ c) stop them.

Activity 2

In small groups, make a list of the virtues of 'Ali Ibn Abee Taalib ﷺ.

Things that Break Wudoo'

Word Bank

nullify,
consciousness
apostasy

What are the things that break *wudoo'*?

- There are certain acts that break *wudoo'*. If a Muslim does any of these acts she/he will need to perform *wudoo'* again.

- Some of the things that nullify *wudoo'* are:

1- Anything that comes out of the two passages (urine, stool, wind) .

2- Excessive bleeding.

3- Losing consciousness, during sleep or otherwise .

4- Apostasy- Leaving Islam.

5- Eating camel meat.

- There are many things that do not nullify *wudoo'*. Here is a list of things that some people think may break *wudoo'* but in fact do not:

  1- Eating or drinking
  2- Laughing
  3- Vomiting

  4- Changing a baby's diaper, without touching the baby's private parts.
  5- Talking while making *wudoo'*

What does 'nullify' mean?

Activity 1

In pairs or small groups, list the things that nullify *wudoo'*.

_____

_____

_____

_____

Activity 2

Discuss the things that people think may break *wudoo'* while in fact they do not break *wudoo'*.

Review
Soorah al-Mutaffifeen (Part 1& 2)
and Soorah al-Inshiqaaq (Parts 1& 2)

1- In this period, your teacher will test you on the *soorahs* you have learned.

You will be tested on the following:

- Recitation and memorization of the above-mentioned *soorahs*.

- To know whether you have a basic idea of the meanings of the above-mentioned *soorahs*.

2- While your teacher tests some of the students individually, practice the following:

- Sit in pairs.
- Recite the soorahs to each other.
- Correct each other's mistakes.
- Recite the *soorahs* again and try to limit the mistakes.
- Once you know one *soorah* perfectly, proceed to the next one.
- Revise the meanings of the *soorahs* and try to memorize them perfectly.

Unit 12

- Some Rulings on *Wudoo'*

- Acts of Worship and *Wudoo'*

- *Soorah al-Infitaar:*
  The Cleaving (Part 1)

Some Rulings on Wudoo'

Word Bank

certainty

doubt

taahir (pure)

mus-haf

(text of the *Qur'aan*)

defecating

This lesson will give some rulings on *wudoo'*.

- If a Muslim is praying and thinks he may have broken wind, but is not sure, is his *wudoo'* nullified? No, because Allah's Messenger ﷺ said,

"If one of you feels something in his stomach and is not sure if he has broken wind or not, he should not leave the masjid until he hears or smells something." (Muslim)

- Feelings and sounds that are felt and heard from a person's stomach due to digesting food does not break *wudoo'*. The person remains *taahir*. Having doubts does not mean that a person is not *taahir*. His *wudoo'* will only break when he is certain that he has broken wind.

- Yet if a person is not sure if his *wudoo'* has been nullified and he is in doubt, there is no problem if *wudoo'* is performed again. Prophet Muhammad ﷺ said,

> *"Leave that which makes you doubtful for that which does not make you doubtful."* (Nasaa'i; Tirmidhi, and Haakim)

- If a Muslim falls asleep and does not know if his *wudoo'* has been broken or not, *wudoo'* should be made again. Safwaan Ibn 'Assaal ؓ reported that the Prophet ﷺ said that *wudoo'* should be made: *"...for defecating, urinating, and sleep."* (Al-Bukhaari)

- If a Muslim does not have *wudoo'* and wants to touch the *mus-haf* of the *Qur'aan*, he should first make *wudoo'*.
Allah's Messenger ﷺ wrote a letter to 'Amr Ibn Hazm ؓ saying,

> *"No one should touch the Qur'aan except the purified."* [Daarimi]

Answer the questions:

1- **If** a Muslim is praying and feels something turning in his stomach, is his *wudoo'* nullified?

No, because the prophet muhamed sal "if one of you feels something in his stomaee and is not pure if he had Broken wind or not he should not leave the masjid until he hears or smells something.

2- **How** are things ruled to remain *taahir*?

Feelings and sounds that are felt and heard from a person's stomace. The person Remains taahir. having dabous dose not mean that a person is not tahir.
No wodo...

3- **Does** doubt (whether you have *wudoo'*) break one's *wudoo'*?

Yes if a person is not sure his wodu has been nullfied and he is in douby there is no problem if woodu is Performed again.

Activity 1

Look at 'Abdullaah and Daawood:

1- **What** is happening in the pictures above?

In the first one he's thinking if he
did woodo in the seccond one he remembered
he did woodo in the 3rd one he's sleepring in

2- **What** are the rulings on each one and
what should they do?

The y one
he woke
up

for one and two if you dont know
you have woodu then you need to make it
In 3 and 4 when you sleep _when_
you wake up You have to make woodu.

Activity 2

Choose the correct answers:

1- **Prophet** Muhammad ﷺ said:

☐ a) "Leave that which makes you certain for that which does not make you certain."

☐ b) "Leave that which does not make you doubtful for that which makes you doubtful."

☑ c) "Leave that which makes you doubtful for that which does not make you doubtful."

2- **Prophet** Muhammad ﷺ said that *wudoo'* should be made:

☑ a) "…for defecating, urinating, and sleep."

☐ b) "…for defecating, eating, and sleep."

☑ c) "…for defecating, and urinating."

3- **Allah's** Messenger ﷺ wrote a famous letter to 'Amr Ibn Hazm ﷺ saying;

☐ a) "Everyone should touch the *Qur'aan* except the purified."

☑ b) "No one should touch the *Qur'aan* except the purified."

☐ c) "No one should touch the *Qur'aan* at all."

Acts of Worship and Wudoo'

Word Bank

status
the *Sahaabah*
(Companions)

Muslims have to perform wudoo' before they perform certain acts of worship

Allah ﷻ says,

"Indeed, Allah loves those who are constantly repentant and loves those who purify themselves."
(Soorah al-Baqarah: 222)

- When Muslims worship Allah ﷻ they make sure that they are clean and have *wudoo'*. This is because Allah ﷻ loves those who turn to Him while they are in a state of *wudoo'*.
- There are certain acts of worship that need *wudoo'*.

> "Shall I suggest to you that by which Allah ﷻ wipes out sins and raises people's status?" They (the Sahaabah) said: "Yes, Messenger of Allah ﷺ He said: "Perform wudoo properly, even in difficulty."
>
> (Muslim)

- Making *wudoo'* when it is difficult can include making *wudoo'* when it is cold or when one is sick.

- Muslims have to make *wudoo'* if they want to perform any of the following acts of worship:

Tawaaf   **Salah**   **Touching the Qur'aan**

Answer the questions:

1- **Which** *aayah* of the *Qur'aan* mentions that Allah ﷻ loves those who purify themselves?

Indeed Allah loves those who are consatly repenek and loves those who purify themsdfs.

قال آتعاكروليات الله يحبت التو ابين تحبت الا تطهرين

تعالى

2- **What** did Prophet Muhammad ﷺ say to the *Sahabaah* ﷺ about wudoo'?

Shall i sugget to you that by wich allah ✓ wipes out sins and rases pepole stats They the sbbhannah said yes messenyer of allah he said perform woodu pryply even in difuclty.

Maha Ahmed

Activity 1

In pairs, find the acts of worship that require Muslims to perform *wudoo'*.

Touching the *hadeeth*	✗
Salah	
Listening to the *Qur'aan*	✗
Making *Tawaaf* around the Ka'bah	
Sawm	✗
Giving *Zakah*	✗
Giving *Sadaqah*	✗
Saying the *Shahaadah*	✗
Touching the *Qur'aan*	

Red means No!
Pink means yes!

Activity 2

$\frac{45}{15}$

Choose the correct answers:

1- Performing *wudoo'* is a great virtue that:

- ☐ a) Only wipes away sins
- ☐ b) Only raises people's status
- ☑ c) Wipes away sins and raises people's status
- ☐ d) Wipes away dirt and raises people's hands,

2- The Messenger of Allah ﷺ said: *"Perform wudoo' properly even in difficulty."* This *hadeeth* shows the importance of performing *wudoo'* even if there is:

- ☐ a) Water
- ☑ b) Difficulty
- ☐ c) Ease
- ☐ d) A person

3- Muslims have to make *wudoo'* if they want to do any of these acts:

- ☐ a) Eat
- ☐ b) Give *sadaqah*
- ☑ c) *Salah*
- ☑ d) Touch the *Qur'aan*
- ☐ e) Play

Soorah al-Infitaar:
The Cleaving (Part 1)

Word Bank

gathered
emptied

This part of the *soorah* shows some of the events that will occur on the Day of Judgment.

Soorah al-Infitaar

Bismillaahir-Rahmaanir-Raheem

بِسْمِ اللّٰهِ الرَّحْمٰنِ الرَّحِيْمِ

1. When the sky breaks apart

إِذَا السَّمَآءُ انفَطَرَتْ ﴿١﴾

2. And when the stars fall, scattering,

وَإِذَا الْكَوَاكِبُ انتَثَرَتْ ﴿٢﴾

3. And when the seas are erupted

وَإِذَا الْبِحَارُ فُجِّرَتْ ﴿٣﴾

4. And when the [contents of] graves are scattered [i.e., exposed],

وَإِذَا الْقُبُورُ بُعْثِرَتْ ﴿٤﴾

5. A soul will [then] know what it has put forth and kept back.

عَلِمَتْ نَفْسٌ مَّا قَدَّمَتْ

وَأَخَّرَتْ ﴿٥﴾

6. O mankind, what has deceived you concerning your Lord, the Generous, ◄

يَٰٓأَيُّهَا ٱلۡإِنسَٰنُ مَا غَرَّكَ بِرَبِّكَ ٱلۡكَرِيمِ ﴿٦﴾

7. Who created you, proportioned you, and balanced you? ◄

ٱلَّذِى خَلَقَكَ فَسَوَّىٰكَ فَعَدَلَكَ ﴿٧﴾

8. In whatever form He willed has He assembled you. ◄

فِىٓ أَىِّ صُورَةٍ مَّا شَآءَ رَكَّبَكَ ﴿٨﴾

9. No! But you deny the Recompense. ◄

كَلَّا بَلۡ تُكَذِّبُونَ بِٱلدِّينِ ﴿٩﴾

10. And indeed, [appointed] over you are keepers, ◄

وَإِنَّ عَلَيۡكُمۡ لَحَٰفِظِينَ ﴿١٠﴾

(سورة الإنفطار: ١-١٠)

We learn from the soorah

1- On the Day of Judgment, the sky will split into two.

2- The stars in the sky will fall onto the earth.

3- All the seas will be gathered and made into one massive sea.

4- All the graves will be emptied.

5- People will know which of their actions will help them.

Look at verses 7-10 then mention why people should be grateful to Allah ﷻ.

Activity 1

a) **Listen** to the teacher recite the *soorah* and repeat after him/her.

b) **Listen** to a recording of the *soorah* and repeat after each *aayah*.

Activity 2

a) **Recite** this part of the *soorah* in a group.

b) **You** must recite the *soorah* to the teacher.

c) **One** student must recite and the rest of the students repeat after him/her.

Activity 3

Watch a video recording of a recitation of the *soorah* and try to imitate the reciter.

Unit 13

The Time of *Fajr*

Word Bank

true dawn
horizon
fake dawn
vertically

When do Muslims offer the *Fajr* prayer?

- *Fajr* is the first prayer of the day, that Muslims perform.

- *Fajr* is from the time of the true dawn until just before the sun rises.

- As the last portion of the night arrives, fine streaks of light and brightness appear on the horizon. These fine streaks of light appear before the true dawn.

- True dawn is when light spreads in the horizon while the fake dawn is when fine streaks of light spread vertically from the horizon up into the night sky.

- The Prophet ﷺ said, "Whoever catches one rak'ah of *Fajr* prayer before sunrise, has caught the *Fajr* prayer." (Al-Bukhaari)

  Prophet Muhammad ﷺ offered the *Fajr* prayer when it was still dark. (Bukhaari and Muslim)

- The Prophet ﷺ prayed *Fajr* at a time when people could not recognize each other. [Muslim] This shows that it is dark at the time of *Fajr*, and the Prophet ﷺ said that one of the best actions is to pray early. (Al-Bukhaari)

- Muslims do not pray at sunrise.

Exercises!

Answer the questions:

1- What is 'true dawn'?

True dawn comes befor fajir time and true dawn is when the light spread in the horzin.

2- What is 'fake dawn'?

fake dawn is when finc streaks of light spread vertially from the horizon up into the night sky.

Activity 1

What is the time for *Fajr* prayer in your local area and *masjid*?

...6 o.clock.

See if the times are more or less the same as the times which the Prophet Muhammad ﷺ described.

Write down your answers and read it to the class in the next lesson.

The phorphet prayed fajir at a time when pepole could not reconize echother,

Activity 2

Discuss
Should Muslims pray *Fajr* when it is light?

No.

What did Prophet Muhammad ﷺ do?

Phophet muhomed offed their at fajir prayer when it was still dark.

The Time of *Dhuhr*

Word Bank

noon,
zenith
extreme
heat

When do Muslims offer the *Dhuhr* prayer?

- *Dhuhr* (noon) prayer is the second prayer of the day.

- Its time begins when the sun passes its zenith, and extends until when the shadow of an object is equal to its height.

- The zenith is when the sun is at its peak. The time of the zenith changes throughout the year.

- The normal practice of Prophet Muhammad ﷺ was to pray *Dhuhr* when the sun was at its hottest. (Al-Bukhaari)

- However, if it is extremely hot and therefore difficult for people to come for prayer, then it is preferred to delay *dhuhr* until it is cooler, so that Muslims can pray with humility and tranquility.

- The Prophet Muhammad ﷺ said:

> *"When it is hot, delay the prayer until it cools down, because the intense heat is from the fragrance of Hell."*
>
> [Al- Bukhaari and Muslim]

- Anas ﷺ said:

> *"If it was extremely cold, the Prophet ﷺ would still pray early. But if it was extremely hot, he would wait until it cools down"*.
>
> (Al-Bukhaari)

- However, it should not be delayed up until the end of its time.

Answer the questions:

6/10

1- **When** does *Dhuhr* start?

It's time begins when the sun pasees its Zenith and extedens untill when the shondo of an object is equl to its haight

2- **What** does 'zenith' mean?

The zenith is when the sun is at is peack the time of the zenith choges throgh the year.

3- **With** regard to the best time to perform *Dhuhr Salah*, what is preferred when the weather is extremely hot?

When the Wether is hot delly the prayer untill its cold becouse the ince hea is from the fragle hell

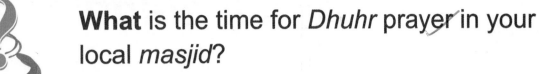

Activity 1

What is the time for *Dhuhr* prayer in your local *masjid*?

12:25

See if the times are more or less the same as the times which the Prophet Muhammad ﷺ described.

It's less then the phrophet, becouse the phrophet time was more

Activity 2

Discuss

In small groups, make notes on the Prophet Muhammad's ﷺ guidance about praying *Dhuhr* when the weather is extremely hot? **Why** is it important to delay *Dhuhr* if the weather is extremely hot and for how long should it be delayed?
Present your findings to the rest of the class.

Unit 13

Lesson 3

Soorah al-Infitaar
The Cleaving (Part 2)

Word Bank

Reckoning

This part of the *soorah* explains that each man has two angels appointed, who write down everything he does.

Soorah al-Infitaar

Bismillaahir-Rahmaanir-Raheem

بِسْمِ اللَّهِ الرَّحْمَٰنِ الرَّحِيمِ

11. Noble and recording;

كِرَامًا كَاتِبِينَ ۝

12. They know whatever you do.

يَعْلَمُونَ مَا تَفْعَلُونَ ۝

13. Indeed, the righteous will be in pleasure,

إِنَّ الْأَبْرَارَ لَفِي نَعِيمٍ ۝

14. And indeed, the wicked will be in Hellfire.

وَإِنَّ الْفُجَّارَ لَفِي جَحِيمٍ ۝

15. They will [enter to] burn therein on the Day of Recompense,

يَصْلَوْنَهَا يَوْمَ الدِّينِ ۝

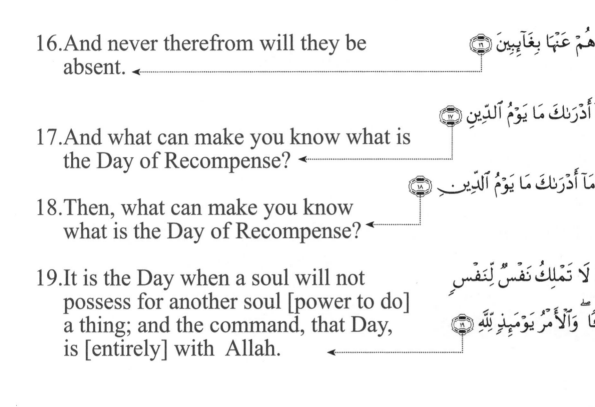

16. And never therefrom will they be absent. ← وَمَا هُمْ عَنْهَا بِغَآئِبِينَ ۝

17. And what can make you know what is the Day of Recompense? ← وَمَآ أَدْرَىٰكَ مَا يَوْمُ ٱلدِّينِ ۝

18. Then, what can make you know what is the Day of Recompense? ← ثُمَّ مَآ أَدْرَىٰكَ مَا يَوْمُ ٱلدِّينِ ۝

19. It is the Day when a soul will not possess for another soul [power to do] a thing; and the command, that Day, is [entirely] with Allah. ← يَوْمَ لَا تَمْلِكُ نَفْسٌ لِّنَفْسٍ شَيْئًا ۖ وَٱلْأَمْرُ يَوْمَئِذٍ لِّلَّهِ ۝

(سورة الإنفطار: ١١-١٩)

We learn from the soorah

1- Some men have disbelieved in the Day of Reckoning.

2- Allah ﷻ has appointed two angels to everyone, who will write down everything they do.

3- Those who are obedient to Allah ﷻ will enter Paradise.

4- Those who are disobedient to Allah ﷻ will enter the blazing Hellfire.

5- All of this will take place on the Day of Judgment.

Exercises!

How does Allah ﷻ describe the Day of Judgment in verse 19 of Soorah al- *Infitaar*?

....

....

....

....

....

Activity 1

a) **Listen** to the teacher recite the *soorah* and repeat after him/her.

b) **Listen** to a recording of the *soorah* and repeat after each *aayah*.

Activity 2

a) **Recite** this part of the *soorah* in a group.

b) **You** must recite the *soorah* to the teacher.

c) **One** student will recite and the rest of the students repeat after him/her.

Activity 3

Watch a video recording of a recitation of the *soorah* and try to imitate the reciter.

Unit 14

- The Time of *'Asr*

- The Time of *Maghrib*

- **Review:**
  Soorah al-Infitaar
  (Parts 1 & 2)

The Time of 'Asr

Word Bank

shadow
undesirable

When do Muslims pray the 'Asr prayer?

- *'Asr* is the middle prayer of the day and is performed in the mid-afternoon.

- *'Asr* can be performed from the time when the *shadow* of an object is equal to its height, until just before the sun sets.

- It is undesirable to pray *'Asr* when the sun is a yellow color, which is just before sunset.

● Prophet Muhammad ﷺ said:

> *"The time of 'Asr is until the sunlight becomes yellow."*
>
> (Muslim)

● Aboo Barza Al-Aslami ﵁ narrated that the Prophet Muhammad ﷺ would offer the *'Asr* prayer and after the prayer one of us would return to his house in the farthest end of Madeenah, and arrive when the sun was still hot and bright. (Al-Bukhaari and Muslim)

● *'Asr* should not be delayed until just before sunset.

Answer the questions:

1- **What** is the time of *'Asr*?

Asr is the middle prayer of the day
and is performed in the mid afternoon.
ASr can be performed from the time
when the Shadow of an object is equl
to it's hight untill just befor the sun
sets

2- **Do** the following:
Go outside at the time of *'Asr*.
Measure the shadow of an object and
see if it is equal to the object's height.

I went out of "asr" with
mesureing tape and the object
was equl to the shadow hight.

Activity 1

What is the time for 'Asr prayer in your local *masjid*?

3:15

See if the times are more or less the same as the times which the Prophet Muhammad ﷺ described. Write down your answers and read it to the class in the next lesson.

Time are more then the phrophet. because his were Less

Activity 2

Discuss

Should Muslims pray 'Asr just before sunset?

No, pray asr when asr Starts.

What did Prophet Muhammad ﷺ say and do in this regard?

Phopet Muhommed said the time of asr is until the Sunlight becomes yellow

The Time of *Maghrib*

Word Bank

shafaq
(twilight)

When do Muslims offer the *Maghrib* prayer?

- *Maghrib* is prayed immediately after sunset.

- The time for *Maghrib* starts when the sun's disc disappears into the horizon, until the red *twilight* is gone.

- The Prophet Muhammad ﷺ said, "*Maghrib* time is as long as the twilight is present." *[Muslim]*

- Twilight is the redness on the western horizon in the evening after sunset.

- Twilight in Arabic is *shafaq*.

Exercises!

Answer the questions:

1- **When** does *Maghrib* start?

Maghirlb is prayed imidle after sunset,

2- **What** does 'twilight' mean ?

twighlight is the reedhees on the western horizons until the red twighly is gene

3- **What** is 'twilight' in Arabic?

Shafaq

Activity 1

What is the time for *Maghrib* prayer in your local *masjid*?

....

See if the times are more or less the same as the times which the Prophet Muhammad ﷺ described. Write down your answers and read it to the class in the next lesson.

....

....

Activity 2

Choose the correct answers:

1- *Maghrib* is prayed immediately:

☐ a) before sunset.

☐ b) after the horizon.

✓ ☑ c) after sunset.

☐ d) before the horizon.

2- **Twilight** is the:

☐ a) color on the horizon before sunset.

✓ ☐ b) redness on the eastern horizon in the evening after sunset.

☐ c) redness on the western horizon in the evening before sunset.

☑ d) redness on the western horizon in the evening after sunset.

✓ 3- **In** Arabic 'twilight' is:

☐ a) *wasaq.*

☐ b) *tasaq.*

☐ c) tabaq.

☐ d) *nafaq.*

☑ e) *shafaq.*

Review
Soorah al- Infitaar (Parts 1 & 2)

1- **In** this period, your teacher will test you on the *soorahs* you have learned.

You will be tested on the following:

- Recitation and memorization of the above-mentioned *soorahs*.

- To know whether you have a basic idea of the meanings of the above-mentioned *soorahs*.

2- **While** your teacher tests some of the students individually, practice the following:
Sit in pairs.
Recite the *soorahs* to each other.
Correct each other's mistakes.
Recite the *soorahs* again and try to limit the mistakes.
Once you know one soorah perfectly, proceed to the next one.
Revise the meanings of the *soorahs* and try to memorize them perfectly.